Spiritual Renewal

Spiritual Renewal

Transforming the Mind

By
Bob Perry

iUniverse, Inc.
New York Lincoln Shanghai

Spiritual Renewal
Transforming the Mind

iUniverse, Inc.

For information address:
iUniverse, Inc.
2021 Pine Lake Road, Suite 100
Lincoln, NE 68512
www.iuniverse.com

ISBN: 0-595-32179-8 (pbk)
ISBN: 0-595-66489-X (cloth)

Printed in the United States of America

Contents

To the Reader, from the Author

Some feel man's imagination creates the idea of God and that God is just that—an idea, a superstition, an antiquated way of dealing with the unknown. Most, however, have faith in God. Even those who hesitate to identify with organized religion believe in some type of higher power. They believe in some presence with the ability to create something from nothing; a Supreme Being providing order and balance to the universe in which we exist. This Supreme Being we describe as God is the source of hope, happiness, peace of mind, and renewal of the spirit.

The viewpoints expressed in this book may be unlike other religious writings because my background differs from most other spiritual writers. Organized religion and the ministry are not my profession, but I do have some credentials in speaking about spiritual affairs. Graduating from a Christian university with a heavy emphasis on biblical study helped prepare me to speak to groups as a lay minister and serve as a deacon in a local congregation. Teaching adult Bible classes for over 22 years has given me the opportunity to spend thousands of hours discussing spiritual issues with people seeking a spiritually fulfilled life.

My professional career, however, has been devoted to organizational development and helping groups improve leadership, management techniques, and performance. I have discovered many people are interested in the spiritual aspects of their lives, even though they do not associate with a religious group. There are surprising similarities between building a dynamic business organization and a spiritual church. Both groups rely on encouraging people to function effectively. The two groups also need people who can continually improve themselves. I find spiritually centered people are better equipped to adapt and overcome life's challenges. This book will share some of the lessons learned from people who have achieved success as well as those who have struggled with life.

We will explore innovative and fresh perspectives about spiritual renewal. In a straightforward way, we will attempt to explain how to develop meaning and purpose in your life. Some ideas offered in this book will be easy to accept since they affirm feelings about spirituality you already possess. Other concepts may be more problematic because they differ from prevalent views many have about religion, Christianity, and spirituality. You will be challenged to have an open mind, think, and explore the truth about spirituality for yourself.

This examination of spiritual renewal uses many quotations from the Bible. The Bible is the best insight we have into God's nature. The Bible is perhaps the most ancient, most read, the most interesting, and possibly the most misunderstood narrative ever written. Have the courage to read, reflect, and discover the Bible with an open mind. It is the story of man's relationship with God.

Be cautious about taking bits and pieces of the Bible out of context. Since the Bible is the most read and most studied book in history, chapter breaks and numbered verses have been added to help locate ideas and specific passages. This is a great study aid; but the Bible uses words, sentences, and paragraphs to express ideas. To help discover the true meaning of a specific verse, try examining several verses before and after the passage you are contemplating.

If you rely on one verse or one specific translation of a scripture to establish religious truth, you may not be getting the most out of God's message to you. The Bible is written like a finely woven tapestry that comes together to make something interesting and beautiful. The ideas and concepts are repeated and consistent. Even the story of Jesus Christ is told from four separate perspectives. Good luck on your quest for spiritual renewal.

The Need for Renewal

"…like grass which is renewed in the morning:
in the morning it flourishes and is renewed;
in the evening it fades and withers."

—David, Psalms 90:5, 6

What would life be like if we were never tired, always alert, full of vigor, and ready to tackle all of life's problems? It would be great! We would enjoy a tireless flow of energy while our health, temperament, finances, relationships, and accomplishments would all improve.

Unfortunately, we are more often tired and worn out. We often lack the energy to effectively deal with the many challenges of life. In the physical sense, we deal with fatigue sometimes to the point of exhaustion. We look forward to the weekend, a vacation, or maybe just a good night's rest to help recharge our batteries. We need physical renewal on a regular basis, but many also need renewal of the spirit. The problems of life beat down and beat up some people. They never feel re-energize or refreshed while despair, hopelessness, and apathy become their perpetual mindset.

Achieving physical renewal becomes more difficult as we mature into adulthood. We tire more easily, our muscles ache when overextended, and sleep becomes more elusive. At some point, most of us recognize the temporary nature of the physical bodies in which we exist.

The writer of the *Letter to the Romans* advised, *"Do not be conformed to this world but be transformed by the renewal of your mind."*[1] Fatigue is often as much a mental feeling as it is a physical condition. Spiritual renewal begins with transforming the mind. By learning to think differently and more positively, we can achieve more peace of mind, more energy, and more satisfaction in life. Joy, hope, peace, happiness, and a brighter future can be yours. The ability to be spiritually renewed is within you right now!

The logic, reason, and the rational thinking ability of humankind is a marvelous capability. We have developed knowledge, technology, and expertise to solve a myriad of life's questions. Humankind is the only creature in the physical world with the ability to process ideas, develop theories, and synthesize information. We alone have the power to imagine and invent things that do not currently exist.

Yet with all this knowledge and expertise, we still struggle with the real questions of life. Where did we come from? How did something come from nothing? What started it all? When was the beginning? The same seemingly unanswerable questions perplex all of us. What does it all mean? Why am I here? Is there a purpose to life and if so, what is it? Trying to know the spiritual God in the physical world is perhaps the essence of a renewed spirit and a transformed mind. Understanding the omnipresent, omniscient, and almighty God (a presence not bound by the constraints of time, space, or dimension) by mortal men and women is a daunting task.

Understanding spirituality becomes confusing because we experience and exist in the physical world. Our hope, however, is for a bet-

---

1.   Romans 12:2, Revised Standard Version of The Bible

ter existence. Jesus once said, *"It is the spirit that gives life, the flesh is of no avail."*[2] Logic dictates that our physical existence is limited, but the power of the mind and the hope of a spiritual existence help sustain countless people through good times and bad. I am convinced spiritual renewal is possible and can make your life better. We have the power inside of us to renew the spirit by transforming the mind, but we must know how.

Discovering purpose and meaning in life is a powerful step in becoming spiritually mature. Transforming the mind to think beyond the constraints of the physical world and toward a promise of a more meaningful existence involves the *power of belief,* the *responsibility to choose,* and the *opportunity to change.* These essential elements of spiritual renewal can be easily learned, but only you can unleash the power and energy of spiritual renewal within you.

Application

Belief is powerful. Confidence in yourself and optimism in your abilities permit you to be innovative, successful, self-reliant, empathic, and humble. Being a mature, poised, and assured person requires strong self-assurance. One way to become more self-assured is to have an even greater faith in a higher power. A belief in God as the creator of the universe and a faith that we are made in his image is a good reason to feel self-assured. As David proclaimed, *"I am fearfully and wonderfully made."*[3]

We also have responsibility and authority for the choices we make. Until we are willing to accept responsibility for our actions, spiritual renewal is not possible. When we blame others, worry, and

---

2.   John 6:63, Revised Standard Version of The Bible
3.   Psalms 139:14, King James Version of The Bible

complain about our circumstances, we are not accepting this responsibility. You are empowered to choose your actions and your attitude. If you are feeling resentful, worried, cynical, anxious, timid,
apathetic, or angry, it is your choice. The transformed mind fills
with optimism, hope, tolerance, and contentment, because thinking
positively is a choice.

Besides tapping into the power of belief and accepting the
responsibility to choose, the opportunity to change becomes a great
tool for spiritual renewal. How dismal life would be, if we were not
able to learn from past mistakes. The great gift from God is the
chance to alter the direction of our lives and begin again on a positive path. Use the rest of this book as an opportunity to think about
how you can use

The Power of Belief,
Responsibility to Choose, and
Opportunity to Change!

The Importance of Purpose and Meaning

"I denied myself nothing my eyes desired; I refused my heart no pleasure. My heart took delight in all my work, and this was the reward for all my labor. Yet when I surveyed all that my hands had done and what I had toiled to achieve, everything was meaningless, a chasing after the wind; nothing was gained under the sun."

—Solomon, Ecclesiastes 2:10, 11

The word *WHY* is a question of purpose. It is perhaps the most intriguing and most perplexing question humankind has faced throughout history. *WHY* is a question of motivations and of reasoning, yet the question *WHY* is sometimes difficult to answer in the physical, material, and finite world in which we exist. The existential philosopher Friedrich Nietzsche addressed the importance of purpose by writing, "If you have a *WHY* in your life, you can deal with almost any *HOW*."

The above passage form *Ecclesiastes*, written about the great king Solomon, could well describe the materialistic culture in which we live. **In an age of unparalleled wealth and prosperity, many live in utter despair.** No point in time has ever provided more economic opportunity, more leisure, or more luxury for the masses than the current age. We deny ourselves "nothing our eyes desire" and deny ourselves few "pleasures." We work hard, accomplish, and achieve, but still there seems to be something missing in the lives of many.

Solomon

Solomon is said to have *"excelled all the kings of the earth in riches and wisdom."*[1] He accomplished great things, denied himself no pleasure, had great wealth, and was blessed with wisdom, power, riches, and influence. Solomon was the major influence and author of three Biblical books, the *Song of Solomon*, *Proverbs*, and *Ecclesiastes*. These three books reflect Solomon's attitude and thinking at different periods of his life.

The *Song of Solomon* is a youthful book brimming with romance and hope. The writing is rich in imagery and filled with beautiful descriptions of the material surroundings.

Proverbs could be described as Solomon's middle-age book, packed with practical wisdom. The short, pithy sayings are powerful instruction on how to live life financially, socially, morally, successfully, and spiritually.

Ecclesiastes, however, is a more distressing and perplexing work. This writing expresses Solomon's questioning about the purpose of life. Whereas the *Song of Solomon* characterizes hope and *Proverbs* epitomizes practical wisdom, the book of *Ecclesiastes* is cynical and filled with despair.

Ecclesiastes reads like a mid-life crisis, a search for the meaning of life by a man who has everything, yet wonders what it all means. The word or idea "vanity of vanities" (other translations use the

---

1.   I Kings 10:23, Revised Standard Version of The Bible

word meaningless) is used over 35 times in the short book of *Ecclesiastes*. The opening passage of *Ecclesiastes* states the book's theme, *"Vanity of vanities, says the Preacher, vanity of vanities! **All is vanity.** What does man gain by all the toil at which he toils under the sun?"*[2]

Ecclesiastes desperately explores the meaning and purpose of life. The book rants about the meaninglessness and vanity of human wisdom, of philosophy, of disappointing experiences, of wealth, and of honor. It describes the torment of a life without purpose. After examining the meaninglessness of life, the writer of *Ecclesiastes* concludes the only purpose of man is to believe and revere God, and obey his will. The closing thoughts of *Ecclesiastes* conclude Solomon's deep searching with a bold statement about the purpose of humankind, and the meaning of life. *"The end of the matter; all has been heard. Fear God, and keep his commandments; for this is the whole duty of man."*[3]

Like Solomon, we have toiled, worked, and labored to attain comfort, pleasure, and physical delight only to find that *"all is vanity and a striving after wind."*[4] Suicide, alcoholism, drug abuse, and depression are serious problems facing society today. In the United States, about 29,000 people commit suicide each year. Approximately 86 people a day or one person every 18 minutes finds life so hopeless that they take their own life. Suicide is the 11th leading cause of death. Among college students, suicide is the second leading cause of death, and for people age 15–24 suicide is the third leading cause of death.[5] These horrific social problems come from

---

2. Ecclesiastes 1:2, 3, Revised Standard Version of The Bible
3. Ecclesiastes 12:13, Revised Standard Version of The Bible
4. Ecclesiastes 1:14, Revised Standard Version of The Bible
5. American Foundation for Suicide Prevention, http://www.afsp.org

feelings of hopelessness, helplessness, or worthlessness; a basic failure to find meaning and purpose in life.

Tolstoy

Leo Nikolayevich Tolstoy, (1883–1911) Russian philosopher and author of *War and Peace*, faced a crisis of purpose at the height of his literary career in the mid 1870's. Tolstoy endured a period of profound doubt and moral searching about the purpose of his life. At the time, he had everything for which to live. He seemed to have an ideal wife, the perfect mother of his children, the mistress of his household, and an invaluable assistant in his literary labors. Tolstoy's estate was thriving, and his published fiction had brought him worldwide renown. Celebrity, success, and periods of family happiness, however, did not equate to peace of mind for Tolstoy. At the height of his fame and fortune, he found life meaningless and openly talked about the difficulty he faced in not taking his own life.

In his quest for the meaning of life, Tolstoy found little help in the works of theologians, philosophers, and scientists, which he systematically examined. However, the peasants, a Russian class of people for whom he always held the greatest empathy, did give him a clue. When he asked them to explain their way of life, they told him that one must serve God and not live for oneself.

Tolstoy next turned to a self-study of the Bible, especially the New Testament. In the teaching of Christ, Tolstoy believed he found answers to his questions. "There is a power in each of us," he declared, "which enables us to discern what is good, and we are in touch with that power. God is that power. Our reason and conscience flow from it, and the purpose of our conscious life is to do his will, that is, to do good."[6]

The story of his moral and spiritual suffering, which brought him to the brink of suicide in his search for a satisfactory explanation of the meaning of his life, is told with compelling power in *A Confession,* written in 1878–1879. Tolstoy chronicled his feelings of apathy and despair about his life as well as his quest for spiritual purpose.

> My lapse from faith occurred as is usual among people on our level of education. I think very many people have had a like experience. With all my soul I wished to be good, but I was young, passionate and alone, completely alone when I sought goodness. Every time I tried to express my most sincere desire, which was to be morally good, I met with contempt and ridicule, but as soon as I yielded to low passions, I was praised and encouraged. **Ambition, love of power, covetousness, lasciviousness, pride, anger, and revenge—were all respected.**
>
> I cannot think of those years without horror, loathing and heartache. I killed men in war and challenged men to duels in order to kill them. I lost at cards, consumed the labor of the peasants, sentenced them to punishments, lived loosely, and deceived people. Lying, robbery, adultery of all kinds, drunkenness, violence, murder—there was no crime I did not commit, and in spite of that people praised my conduct and my contemporaries considered and consider me to be a comparatively moral man.
>
> **My life came to a standstill.** I could breathe, eat, drink, and sleep, and I could not help doing these things; but there was no life, for there were no wishes the fulfillment of which I could consider reasonable. It had come to this, that I, a healthy, fortunate man, felt I could no longer live: some irresistible power impelled me to rid myself one way or another of life. I cannot say I "wished" to kill myself. The power, which drew me away from life was stronger, fuller, and more widespread than any mere

---

6.   Tolstoy, Leo Nikolayevich, A Confession, 1879, Russia

wish. It was a force similar to the former striving to live, only in a contrary direction. All my strength drew me away from life. The thought of self-destruction now came to me as naturally as thoughts of how to improve my life had come formerly. It was seductive and I had to be cunning with myself lest I should carry it out too hastily. It was then that I, a man favored by fortune, hid a cord from myself lest I should hang myself from the cross-piece of the partition in my room where I undressed alone every evening, and I ceased to go out shooting with a gun lest I should be tempted by so easy a way of ending my life.

I did not myself know what I wanted: I feared life, desired to escape from it, yet still hoped something of it. All this befell me at a time when all around me I had what is considered complete good fortune. I was not yet fifty; I had a good wife who loved me and whom I loved, good children, and a large estate which with-out much effort on my part improved and increased. I was respected by my relations and acquaintances more than at any previous time. I was praised by others and without much self-deception could consider that my name was famous. Far from being insane or mentally diseased, I enjoyed on the contrary a strength of mind and body such as I have seldom met with among men of my kind; physically I could keep up with the peas-ants at mowing, and mentally I could work for eight and ten hours at a stretch without experiencing any ill results from such exertion. In this situation I came to this—that I could not live, and, fearing death, had to employ cunning with myself to avoid taking my own life.

I sought everywhere; and thanks to a life spent in learning, and thanks also to my relations with the scholarly world, I had access to scientists and scholars in all branches of knowledge, and they readily showed me all their knowledge, not only in books but also in conversation, so that I had at my disposal all that sci-ence has to say on this question of life. If one turns to the branches of science which are not concerned with the solution of the questions of life, but which reply to their own special scientific questions, one is enraptured by the power of man's mind, but one knows in advance that they give no reply to life's questions.

The simplest laboring people around me were the Russian people, and I turned to them and to the meaning of life, which they give. That meaning, if one can put it into words, was as follows: **Every man has come into this world by the will of God and God has so made man that every man can destroy his soul or save it.** The aim of man in life is to save his soul, and to save his soul he must live "godly" and to live "godly" he must renounce all the pleasures of life, must labor, humble himself, suffer, and be merciful.

Faith is the strength of life. If a man lives, he believes in something. If he did not believe that one must live for something, he would not live. Without faith he cannot live. If I exist, there must be some cause for it, and a cause of causes. The first cause of all is what men have called "God." I paused on that thought, and tried with all my being to recognize the presence of that cause. **As soon as I acknowledged that there is a force in whose power I am, I at once felt that I could live.** "Live seeking God, and then you will not live without God." More than ever before, all within me and around me lit up, and **the light did not again abandon me.**[7]

Tolstoy's story of self-discovery and searching for a meaning to life is strikingly similar to Solomon's quest for purpose in *Ecclesiastes*. Instead of dealing with failure and poverty, both men struggled to find meaning and purpose to lives filled with accomplishment, notoriety, material comfort, and wealth. Success in the physical world

---

7.   Tolstoy, Leo Nikolayevich, A Confession, 1879, Russia

without purpose and a spiritual meaning made life seem futile to them. Tolstoy described his spiritual renewal in this way.

What happened to me was something like this: I was put into a boat and pushed off from an unknown shore, shown the direction of the opposite shore, had oars put into my unpracticed hands, and was left alone. I rowed as best I could and moved forward; but the further I advanced towards the middle of the stream the more rapid grew the current bearing me away from my goal and the more frequently did I encounter others, like myself, borne away by the stream.

There were a few rowers who continued to row, there were others who had abandoned their oars; there were large boats and immense vessels full of people. Some struggled against the current, others yielded to it. The further I went the more, seeing the progress down the current of all those who were adrift, I forgot the direction given me. In the very center of the stream, amid the crowd of boats and vessels, which were being borne down stream, I quite lost my direction and abandoned my oars. Around me on all sides, with mirth and rejoicing, people with sails and oars were borne down the stream, assuring me and each other that no other direction was possible. I believed them and floated with them. I was carried far; so far that I heard the roar of the rapids in which I must be shattered, and I saw boats shattered in them. I recollected myself. I was long unable to understand what had happened to me. I saw before me nothing but destruction, towards which I was rushing and which I feared. I saw no safety anywhere and did not know what to do; but, looking back, I perceived innumerable boats, which unceasingly and strenuously pushed across the stream, and I remembered about the shore, the oars, and the direction, and began to pull back upwards against the stream and towards the shore.

That shore was God; that direction was tradition; the oars were the freedom given me to pull for the shore and unite with

God. So the force of life was renewed in me and I again began to live.[8]

Tolstoy's quaint description of his journey through spiritual apathy, spiritual searching, and then spiritual renewal gives many clues that the teachings of Jesus were paramount in his discovery of spiritual purpose.

Jesus said, *"…the gate is wide and the way is easy, that leads to destruction, and those who enter by it are many. For the gate is narrow and the way is hard, that leads to life, and those who find it are few."* [9]

Tolstoy's analogy of his trip down the river indicated that it was filled with others who were floating and taking what seemed to be the easy way through life. There is a perceived comfort and safety in numbers. One challenge in finding spiritual renewal is breaking the force of the status quo and finding faith in the higher being, by having faith in God.

Application

Purpose is a driving force for a person, particularly in times of stress. Thoughts of self-doubt and struggles with defining a purpose in life are common. Traumatic events often throw us into a feeling of chaos and despair.

These are typical feelings based on secular intellect, wisdom, and experience. Life, in a physical sense, is terminal. This can leave one feeling depressed, meaningless, and hopeless. *"To set the mind on the flesh is death, but to set the mind on the Spirit is life and peace."*[10]

8.　Tolstoy, Leo Nikolayevich, A Confession, 1879, Russia
9.　Matthew 7:13, Revised Standard Version of The Bible
10.　Romans 8:6, Revised Standard Version of The Bible

Spiritual renewal begins with an acceptance of a higher power. A person must believe, rely, and have faith in God as the creator of the universe, as the Father. One vital step in spiritual renewal,

Establish God as your Purpose.

Searching for Spirituality

"That which is born of flesh is flesh, and that which is born of the Spirit is spirit."

—Jesus, John 3:6

Spirituality is something many are searching for and possibly everyone seeks at some point in their life. Spirituality, however, is an almost impossible idea to describe or define. The difficulty in explaining spirituality lies in the ethereal, mysterious, and intangible nature of spirituality.

We live and experience daily the material, tangible, finite nature of the physical world. The five basic senses of sight, hearing, touch, taste, and smell are used to perceive tangible objects, places, and people. These senses convert direct, physical contacts through nerve endings found in the eyes, ears, and skin to the brain.

Emotional and intellectual senses experience the non-physical aspects of human encounters like feelings, ideas, and even time. The experience of spirituality, however, lies in the realm of faith, *"the assurance of things hoped for, the conviction of things not seen."*[1] Spiritu-

---

1.   Hebrews 11:1, Revised Standard Version of The Bible

ality is the infinite and intangible opposite of the physical world we experience as human beings.

There is a tendency to lump all things not easily understood about humanity under the broad heading of spirituality, without really determining what spirituality is. Spirituality is more than human psychology or a feeling. It is the moral, mental, and immaterial part of humanity, the part hidden and difficult to discern.

A person's character includes the assurance they have in their self worth, the attitude that person has about the things in life happening to them, and finally their actions, which are demonstrations of what they believe and feel. Determining character is problematic because so much of an individual's moral construction is hidden in the person's psychology.

The actions of a person are observable, but the motivations are not. A person's attitude is somewhat apparent in behavior, but hides deeper within a person's psyche than actions. The level of self-assurance a person possesses is almost invisible to an outsider because it is embedded into what they are, who they are, and probably what they have experienced in life.

Deeper in the consciousness of a person lay their essence; the beliefs, values, desires, morals, ideals, and ethics that really determine the character of a person. Spirituality resides in this deepest realm of a person's existence.

Although spirituality is a difficult thing to define, the effects of spiritual degeneration are acute. Feelings of frustration, anxiety, emptiness, and a void of purpose can be devastating to the human psyche.

> "I've been wanting to write to you for a long time but I wasn't sure what I wanted to say. I'm still not sure what I want to say except that…I'm sorry for everything…sorry, sorry, sorry. I really blew it, but I held on as long as I could. I was so stifled it felt like I was dying inside and I was not sure how I could express it. I didn't even know who I was…especially when it came to religion I always felt left out."
>
> —Excerpts of a letter from a friend

This message, sent six months after the break-up of a family very close to me, represents the spiritual anguish many are living with today. The words are from the heart. Phrases like, "I'm sorry for everything," "I was so stifled it felt like I was dying inside," "I didn't like my life," "didn't even know who I was…especially when it came to religion" show something was missing in this person's life. This person was not able to find the answers from family, friends, or religion at the time. They lived with the real life consequences caused by spiritual drifting.

The spiritual aspects of humankind can be camouflaged in a person's behavior and personality. A person is responsible to monitor and detect his or her spiritual purpose, because no one else can observe this part a person's being. Paul wrote of the hidden aspects of human character in his *First Letter to the Corinthians*, *"…we impart a secret and hidden wisdom of God, which God decreed before the ages for our glorification. None of the rulers of this age understood this; for if they had they would not have crucified the Lord of glory. But, as it is written, 'What no eye has seen, nor ear heard, nor the heart of man conceived, what God has prepared for those who love him,' God has revealed* *to us through the Spirit. For the Spirit searches everything, even the depths of God. For what person knows a man's thought **except the spirit of the man which is in him?** So also no one comprehends the thoughts of God except the Spirit of God."[2]*

People can observe our behaviors and actions. They may also be able to predict our attitude and level of self-assurance based on these observations. The inner-self (the essence of a person) is composed of beliefs, ethics, desires, ideals, morals, and values that are hidden far from all but that person and God. "For what person knows a man's thought except the spirit of the man which is in him?" To live spiritually, we must align our inner person with the will of God. *"Now we have received not the spirit of the world, but the Spirit which is from God, that we might understand the gifts bestowed on us by God."[3]*

Application

Great thinkers of the ages, as well as the most common of humankind, have struggled at times with the meaning and purpose of life. Solomon found emptiness and despair in his tremendous material accomplishments, then concluded to "Fear God and keep his commandments, for this is the whole duty of man." Tolstoy concluded, "Faith in God is the strength of life," and "Live seeking God, and then you will not live without God."

Spiritual renewal begins with a focus on purpose, an acceptance of God as the Father and Creator of all things. The next step in spiritual renewal involves reflection of the inner thoughts deep within us. We need to analyze the beliefs, ethics, desires, ideals, morals, and values that motivate us. After establishing God as our purpose, and

---

2.   I Corinthians 2:7-11, Revised Standard Version of The Bible
3.   I Corinthians 2:12, New International Version of The Bible

identifying the gaps between our worldly desires and his spiritual will, we need to,

Align our thoughts with God's will.

First Things First

"...seek first his kingdom and his righteousness,"
—Jesus, Matthew 6:33

We live in a complex and complicated world. There never seems to be enough time for family, for leisure, for ourselves, or for God. We are so caught up in the urgent things in life we often forget the important things of life. The German poet and philosopher Johann Goethe once wrote, "Things which matter most must never be at the mercy of things which matter least." The inability to focus on the truly important things in life becomes a barrier to spiritual health.

One condition preventing a person from finding purpose and meaning to life is anxiety. Fear and worry about the uncertainty of our physical world inhibit a person's ability to live life abundantly. Jesus addressed the problem of anxiety about this physical life in many of his teachings. He provides an effective strategy to deal with worry in his Sermon on the Mount.

Therefore, I tell you, do not be anxious about your life, what you shall eat or what you shall drink, nor about your body, what you shall put on. Is not life more than food, and the body more than clothing? Look at the birds of the air: they neither sow nor reap nor gather into barns, and yet your heavenly Father feeds them. Are you not of more value than they? And which of you by being anxious can add one cubit to his span of life? And why are you anxious about clothing? Consider the lilies of the field, how they grow; they neither toil nor spin; yet I tell you, even Solomon in all his glory was not arrayed like one of these. But if God so clothes the grass of the field, which today is alive and tomorrow is thrown into the oven, will he not much more clothe you, O men of little faith? Therefore do not be anxious, saying, 'What shall we eat?' or 'What shall we drink?' or 'What shall we wear?' For the Gentiles seek all these things; and your heavenly Father knows that you need them all. **But seek first his kingdom and his righteousness, and all these things shall be yours as well.** [1]

Jesus is talking about the essentials of food, drink, and clothing needed for bodily survival. We physically could not exist without these things, yet Jesus is suggesting that we not worry or be anxious about these essentials.

Think of how many non-essential items distract us from spiritual purpose daily...the car, house, and insurance payment...how the lawn looks...if the kids are getting enough playing time in little league...do people like me...will I get promoted at work...will I have to deal with a difficult person or situation. A myriad of urgent items (many of which will not be important one, ten, or certainly fifty years from now) drain our energy and sap our spiritual strength.

The advice of Jesus does not discount the need for the essentials of our physical existence, but it urges believers to "seek first his kingdom and his righteousness." When the important things (seeking God and righteousness) are addressed as a priority, Jesus promises the urgent things "shall be yours as well."

---

1.   Matthew 6:25-33, Revised Standard Version of The Bible

True genius is the ability to transform the complicated into the simple. Jesus Christ was able to consistently transform the complicated issues of human psychology and human existence into simple, concrete ideas that were easy to implement in the lives of believers. Jesus advocated putting first things first and focusing on a spiritual purpose. He tore down the old ideas of God's law being complex and hard to understand, with a new philosophy that was easy to understand, simple to implement, but challenging to master.

Jesus framed his philosophy in the golden rule, which simply stated, *"So whatever you wish that men would do to you, do so to them; for this is the law and the prophets."*[2] People tend to focus on the idealistic principle to "Treat other people the way you would like to be treated," while forgetting the importance Jesus placed on this teaching. He says, **"…this is the law and the prophets."** This concept of service to our fellow man summarizes God's law, according to Jesus.

Jesus was often confronted by the educated, powerful, and influential people of his day. These cunning antagonists often asked problematic questions in an attempt to trap him in the complexity of the law. In one of these episodes, described in the *Gospel of Matthew*, Jesus again takes the opportunity to emphasize the importance of a spirit of love in fulfilling God's law.

> *And one of them, a lawyer, asked him a question, to test him. "Teacher, which is the great commandment in the law?" And he said to him, "You shall love the Lord your God with all your heart, and with all your soul, and with all your mind. This is the great and first commandment. And a second is like it, You shall love your neighbor as yourself. On these two commandments **depend all the law and the prophets.**"*[3]

---

2.   Matthew 7:12, Revised Standard Version of The Bible

The question, "Which is the greatest commandment?" was asked to challenge Jesus and ensnare him in the intricacies of the law. After instructing them about the paramount importance of loving God and the like significance of loving their fellow man, Jesus uses the phrase "...depend all the law and the prophets." Again, he emphasizes that love is the foundation to righteousness, that love is key to finding spiritual purpose.

The pop culture definition of love in our society makes it difficult to comprehend the importance Jesus places on this concept. We tend to think of love as an emotion or a feeling. In the teachings of Jesus, love is not an emotional feeling; it is an attitude, a way of relating to and treating other people.

Jesus taught love as an attitude by saying, *"You have heard that it was said, 'You shall love your neighbor and hate your enemy.' But I say to you, Love your enemies and pray for those who persecute you."*[4] It is hard to imagine Jesus would expect his followers to have an emotional feeling or infatuation with an enemy. He implies, however, that it is possible to develop a loving attitude toward other people, even those we may dislike or find offensive. The love Jesus is talking about and placing as the cornerstone of his teachings is an attitude of respect in dealing with other people.

Love is not an emotion as much as an attitude. It is a state of mind that can be learned and applied to all human relationships, without having affection or infatuation for the other party. An excellent definition of the loving attitude is found in Paul's *First Letter to the Corinthians. "Love is patient and kind; love is not jealous or boastful; it is not arrogant or rude. Love does not insist on its own way; it is not*

---

3. Matthew 22:35-40, Revised Standard Version of The Bible
4. Matthew 5:43,44, Revised Standard Version

irritable or resentful; it does not rejoice at wrong, but rejoices in the right. Love bears all things, believes all things, hopes all things, endures all things." [5]

This passage is often used in a romantic context in weddings, but the definition and conduct applies in dealing with a host of interpersonal situations including interactions with an enemy and persecutor. The passage is a list of what love is and is not.

Definition of Love for I Corinthians, Chapter 13

Love

- Is **patient**
- Is **kind**
- Does **rejoice in the right**
- **Bears** all things
- **Believes** all things
- **Hopes** all things
- **Endures** all things

- Is not **jealous**
- Is not **boastful**
- Is not **arrogant**
- Is not **rude**
- Does not **insist on its own way**
- Is not **irritable**
- Is not **resentful**
- Does not rejoice **at wrong**

Other New Testament writers verify the fundamental and essential quality of this teaching in serving God. *"For the whole law is fulfilled in one word, 'You shall love your neighbor as yourself.'"* [6] This one idea of loving your neighbor as yourself summarizes the whole philosophy of Jesus.

---

5. I Corinthians 13:4-7, Revised Standard Version of The Bible
6. Galatians 5:14, Revised Standard Version of The Bible

The *Book of Romans* details further the premise of Christianity being rooted in a loving attitude by saying, "*Owe no one anything, except to love one another; for he who loves his neighbor **has fulfilled the law**. The commandments, 'You shall not commit adultery, You shall not kill, You shall not steal, You shall not covet,' and any other commandment, are **summed up in this sentence**, 'You shall love your neighbor as yourself.' Love does no wrong to a neighbor; therefore **love is the fulfilling of the law**.*"[7]

The implications for spiritual development, for human relationships, and for a utopian world found in this simple idea from Jesus cannot be overstated. If humankind were able to properly implement this philosophy personally, nationally, and internationally, all conflicts would be resolved. The proper use of these principles would make all other laws obsolete and unnecessary.

When I was a child learning to play sports that required hitting a ball, like baseball, tennis, or golf, the coach would always say, "Keep your eye on the ball." Now the muscles, the timing, the hand-eye coordination, and the strategies involved in playing these games can be complex, but the advice to "keep your eye on the ball" and to focus on the purpose of the game is still a good place to start.

In learning to follow the example of God's son, it is also wise to focus on the basics. Jesus would say developing a loving attitude is **the basic rule** to becoming God centered and spiritually renewed.

Developing a loving attitude involves becoming less selfish and more selfless. Living in the physical world of scarcity and competition, we tend to focus on being selfish. Our reason and instincts tell us, survival of the fittest. The selfish attributes of envy, strife, anger, jealousy, competition, dissensions, and being divisive make perfect

---

7. Romans 13:8-10, Revised Standard Version of The Bible

sense in the physical world. The downside of these tendencies toward a self-sustaining way of life is that they make us feel meaningless, hopeless, and trivial.

Selfishness is perhaps the greatest barrier to spiritual renewal and becoming a more Godly person. We are challenged to transform the mind from the selfish characteristics of humankind in the physical world, to a more selfless, spiritual nature.

The goodness in life comes from God. Selflessness requires us to do the opposite of what the selfish nature is telling us to do. The attributes of love, joy, peace, patience, kindness, goodness, faithfulness, gentleness, and self-control only seem sensible in the spiritual world.

The *Book of Galatians* defines the root causes of selfishness and selflessness. *"I say, walk by the Spirit, and do not gratify the desires of the flesh. For the desires of the flesh are against the Spirit, and the desires of the Spirit are against the flesh; for these are opposed to each other, to prevent you from doing what you would. But if you are led by the Spirit you are not under the law. Now the works of the flesh are plain: fornication, impurity, licentiousness, idolatry, sorcery, enmity, strife, jealousy, anger, selfishness, dissension, party spirit, envy, drunkenness, carousing, and the like. I warn you, as I warned you before, that those who do such things shall not inherit the kingdom of God. But the fruit of the Spirit is love, joy, peace, patience, kindness, goodness, faithfulness, gentleness, self-control; against such there is no law."*[8]

Spiritual renewal begins with purpose. Solomon said fearing (or respecting) God and keeping his commandments was the whole duty of man. Jesus outlines a clear purpose for his followers in the concept of "treating others the way you would liked to be treated."

---

8.   Galatians 5:16-23, Revised Standard Version of The Bible

Jesus affirms that fulfilling the law is a simple, yet difficult matter of developing a loving attitude in our relationships and service to other people.

When we develop an attitude of service and empathy toward those who are created in the image of God, we begin the path toward finding purpose and meaning in God's creation. We move toward building a beneficial relationship with the God the Creator.

Application

"All scripture is inspired by God and profitable for teaching, for reproof, for correction, and for training in righteousness."[9] Spiritual renewal can only come through seeking to know God and following his will having, *"put on the new nature, which is being renewed in knowledge after the image of its creator."*[10]

The Bible is worthy of a lifetime study, but can be overwhelming. It is probably not realistic to think we will fully know the spiritual God living in our physical nature. Jesus Christ, however, has given us a tremendous focal point in trying to live righteously. Treat other human beings with dignity and respect. Focus on becoming more selfless and less selfish by heeding the teachings of Jesus on developing a loving attitude. *"No man has ever seen God; if we love one another, God abides in us and his love is perfected in us."*[11]

Become more selfless and less selfish by developing a loving attitude.

---

9. II Timothy 3:16, Revised Standard Version of The Bible
10. Colossians 3:10, Revised Standard Version of The Bible
11. I John 4:12, Revised Standard Version of The Bible

The Power of Belief Begins with Possibilities

"...nothing shall be impossible unto you."

—Jesus, Matthew 17:20

Belief is a powerful force. It begins with possibilities, matures with purpose, and is unleashed when it stirs passion. Solomon reflected that, *"He has put eternity into man's mind, yet so that he cannot find out what God has done from the beginning to the end."*[1]

The idea of eternal life is a possibility that becomes assurance to those trusting in God and who set God as the purpose and focal point for their lives.

Discovering the possibilities is the beginning of belief. In 18th century circus shows, "flea circuses" were popular. Fleas are tremendous jumpers able to leap 15 feet or more. The insects were trained by being placed in a jar with a transparent lid. The fleas would try to jump away, but they could not, because they hit the top of the container. After a few days, the fleas would be taken out of the jar. They were conditioned to only jump to a certain height. When the insects

---

1. Ecclesiastes 3:11, Revised Standard Version of The Bible

were taken out of the container, their behavior was modified so that they would jump as if still confined to the container. Nothing stopped them from jumping away but their conditioning and their *failure to see the possibilities.*

In these same circuses, elephants were fastened to a stake with a short chain when they were calves. The baby elephant would try to break free but could not. Years later, when the full-grown elephant had the power to easily break free it still would not. All it would have had to do was walk away, the chain was nothing to a full-grown elephant, but it had been conditioned. It would not break free although there was nothing really stopping it. The elephant would stay tied to the stake without trying to break free because *it failed to see the possibilities.*

The same thing happens to people. Psychologists call this type of learning respondent or operant conditioning. People learn to make a particular response to secure positive reinforcement or to escape painful consequences. People have the ability to change this conditioning, yet it is very rare to find a person who exercises this power of free will, which would allow them to control their own destiny. Most people stay confined to the conditioning with which they have been programmed. *They fail to see the possibilities.*

Human beings have reason and imagination, (the ability to envision things that do not presently exist) and create those things in the real world. People have the ability to control their own mind, to utilize that power to imagine the possibilities. Every human being comes into the world by the will of God and God has made human beings so that we can destroy our soul or save it. Many, however, fail to see the possibility of choosing their attitude, their actions, and even their spiritual relationship with God. By conditioning, people sometimes feel they are helpless victims instead of people created in the image of God with the ability to choose.

There was a time when people believed it was impossible to run a four-minute mile. Many excellent athletes felt it was unattainable; the human body was simply not designed to do it. **People failed to see the possibility,** until Roger Banister ran the four-minute mile in 1954. Suddenly many people began to run the four-minute mile. What was stopping them before was a failure to believe, to see the possibilities. People had accepted the belief that it was impossible to run a four-minute mile, the unconscious mind accepted this belief; it therefore was a reality for almost everyone. When one person broke the barrier, it made obvious the possibilities and it gave permission for many others. After Banister, many track and field athletes who discovered the power of possibilities shattered the barrier. The apostle Paul wrote, *"I can do all things in him who strengthens me."*[2] Paul is talking about the power of belief, the power of possibilities.

The power of belief and the power of possibilities can affect groups also. The year 2000 was a special year for the University of Oklahoma football team. This storied football program won its seventh national championship but to many this one was the most special. The 2000 team was not ranked in the top twenty teams in the country at the beginning of the year. They were picked to finish fourth or fifth in their own conference and were thought by no one as a championship contender.

The recent past of this team had included many more failures than successes. Since 1995, they had managed only one winning season. Their record since 1995 had been a dismal 24 wins, 32 losses, and 1 tie. In the 2000 season, the team won all 13 games, a Big

---

2.   Philippians 4:13, Revised Standard Version of The Bible

Twelve conference championship, an Orange Bowl Championship, and the National Championship.

Here are some excerpts from the Sporting News about the season. Notice how important belief is considered for a sports team. "In just two years, (Coach Bob) Stoops has made **believers** of everyone associated with the program."…"He has them **believing** they can win," says Florida State coach Bobby Bowden. "That's where the battle is won."…"The kids **believed** in the scheme because we had a guy who won a championship doing the same thing four years ago," says Brent Venables, Oklahoma's co-defensive coordinator. "They **believed** in us from day one, and that's a credit to Bob and what he has brought to this program." [3] How does an underrated and presumably under-talented team become champions? It comes with hard work and the power of belief, **the power of possibilities.**

Belief, with an emotional commitment, leads to faith and faith leads to good deeds and righteousness. We are challenged to believe in the possibilities. Believing in the spiritual possibilities is difficult because we live in the realm of the finite and the constrained. We live with the perception of limitations because our material and physical world is limited. Tolstoy wrote, "If a person does not see and recognize the illusory nature of the finite, he believes in the finite; **if he understands the illusory nature of the finite, he must believe in the infinite.**" [4]

The perception we live with is temporary, while the promise is eternal. We live in the physical but the possibilities of renewal exist in the spiritual. We live in a state of doom without God but with the

---

3.   Hayes, Mark. "Sooner Rather Than Later", <u>The Sporting News</u>, January, 2001, http://www.sportingnews.com/voices/matt_hayes/20010109.html

4.   Tolstoy, Leo Nikolayevich, A Confession, 1879, Russia

possibilities of hope through Jesus Christ. Our experience is with the limited and the finite but the possibilities are with the infinite, spiritual, eternal, and all-mighty God. Spiritual renewal requires absolute belief in God.

Paul wrote in his *Second Letter to the Corinthians,* "*So we do not lose heart. Though our outer nature is wasting away, our inner nature is being renewed every day. For this slight momentary affliction is preparing for us an eternal weight of glory beyond all comparison, because we look not to the things that are seen but to the things that are unseen; for the things that are seen are transient, **but the things that are unseen are eternal.**"[5]* Our challenge is to look by faith to the yet unseen spiritual promise.

Our reality is material and in a constant state of decline. The physical man or woman is dying more each day. We are renewed day by day inwardly in the spiritual part of humankind. The reality of what can be seen is limited but spiritual renewal occurs when we train ourselves to see the eternal and believe the possibilities. Jesus said, *"It is the spirit that gives life, the flesh is of no avail; the words that I have spoken to you are spirit and life."[6]*

Belief is fundamental to spiritual development and renewal. The most powerful first sentence of any book fact or fiction, ancient or modern, long or short, is *"In the beginning God created the heavens and the earth."[7]* This declaration is the fundamental of man's relationship to God. He is the Creator, the Father of all things. *"By faith we understand that the world was created by the word of God, so that what is seen was made out of things which do not appear."[8]*

---

5. II Corinthians 4:16-18, Revised Standard Version of The Bible
6. John 6:63, Revised Standard Version of The Bible
7. Genesis 1:1, Revised Standard Version of The Bible
8. Hebrews 11:3, Revised Standard Version of The Bible

Moses was peacefully tending the sheep of his father-in-law in the wilderness close to the mountain Horeb when the angel of the LORD appeared to him in a bush burning with fire, yet not consumed. When the physical Moses was confronted by the spiritual God to lead the nation of Israel out of bondage, he asked God how to describe God. *"God said to Moses, 'I AM WHO I AM.'"*[9] We often make the mistake of trying to teach people religion when we should be teaching them GOD IS!

Application

Until a person believes in God, there is no hope of spiritual growth or spiritual peace. Being spiritual is having a purpose; without God there is no purpose, no Christ, no promise of eternal life. Paul declared in his message to the church at Corinth, *"If for this life only we have hoped in Christ, we are of all men most to be pitied."*[10]

Believe in yourself. You are created in the image of God, wonderfully made. Look beyond the finite and toward the infinite nature of the eternal. Overcome the limitations and constraints of the physical existence by transforming the mind to focus on the spiritual possibilities. Say this affirmation to yourself daily,

I can…do all things in him who strengthens me.

---

9.   Exodus 3:14, Revised Standard Version of The Bible
10.   I Corinthians 15:19, Revised Standard Version of The Bible

Overcoming the Barrier of Fear

"Do not fear, only believe."

—Jesus, Mark 5:36

Happiness is contentment and a learned state of being. Paul wrote, *"Not that I complain of want; for I have **learned**, in whatever state I am, to be content. I know how to be abased, and I know how to abound; in any and all circumstances I have **learned** the secret of facing plenty and hunger, abundance and want."*[1] Paul's secret to being content "in any and all circumstances" was a strong purpose, a total faith in Jesus Christ, his teachings, and his promise.

A person's mental contentment is contingent on strong self-assurance, proper attitude, and constructive actions. The cornerstone of contentment is self-assurance that comes with maturity. Being happy and content is a choice that comes from the transformed mind.

The Bible gives humankind a positive affirmation by declaring that God creates us in his image. *"Then God said, 'Let us make man in our image, in our likeness.'"*[2] David said, *"I will praise thee, for I am*

---

1. Philippians 4:11,12, Revised Standard Version of The Bible
2. Genesis 1:26, Revised Standard Version of The Bible

fearfully and wonderfully made."[3] Indeed, made in the image of God we should be self-assured with the knowledge of our value. Trusting in God allows us to have assurance in ourselves, our purpose, and to believe in our ability to accomplish great things.

Positive thoughts help build self-assurance and unleash the power of belief, especially when we believe in God. Belief in God that is so strong it becomes faith focuses our energy on aligning our will with his. The writer to the Christians in Rome asked the question, *"If God be for us, who can be against us?"*[4] Knowing God has promised redemption in eternity gives believers tremendous self-assurance. Life's troubles become temporary inconveniences when we believe in God's promise of eternity.

Constructive affirmations, positive self-talk, and optimistic attitudes help a person build good self-image. However, if positive thoughts help build strong self-confidence, fear is the great enemy and destroyer of a person's assurance. Fear can be a significant barrier to faith, but belief in God can overpower fear. The writer of the *Letter to the Hebrews* defiantly states, *"Hence we can confidently say, 'The Lord is my helper; I will not be afraid; what can man do to me?'"* [5]

Jesus Christ's disciples cried out in fear when they saw him walking on the water and Jesus said to them, *"...Take courage! It is I. Don't be afraid."*[6] Another time Jesus was ministering to a ruler of the synagogue who was in despair and feared that his child was dead and again Jesus said *"...Do not fear, only believe."*[7]

---

3.   Psalms 139:14, King James Version of The Bible
4.   Romans 8:31, King James Version of The Bible
5.   Hebrews 13:6, Revised Standard Version of The Bible
6.   Matthew 14:2, New International Version of The Bible
7.   Mark 5:36, Revised Standard Version of The Bible

Jesus, of course, knew the power of belief and the tremendous possibilities available through God. He also knew how destructive worry and fear are to belief. Jesus taught, *"Therefore I tell you, do not be anxious about your life, what you shall eat or what you shall drink, nor about your body, what you shall put on. Is not life more than food, and the body more than clothing?"*[8] Jesus encouraged his disciples to prioritize and focus their lives. Jesus goes on to say, *"But seek first his kingdom and his righteousness, and all these things will be given to you as well."* [9]

Spirituality could be equated with a person's understanding of their purpose. Christ teaches that our purpose is to seek or focus on the spiritual kingdom and righteousness. If we take care of the significant things, the routine things of life will take care of themselves.

We live in complex times with many responsibilities to balance. It seems as if everything is changing at an overwhelming pace. Fear and worry easily engulf many people, making life a tedious endeavor.

Jesus presents a highly effective strategy in dealing with anxiety, worry, and fear when he says, *"Therefore do not be anxious about tomorrow, for tomorrow will be anxious for itself. Let the day's own trouble be sufficient for the day."*[10] He encourages followers to live one day at a time. We cannot change the past, only learn from it. Worrying about the future will change nothing; we can only plan and prepare for it. We can, however, take control of and take advantage of the opportunities present each day.

In 1935, two recovered alcoholics, William Griffith and Robert Holbrook, established Alcoholics Anonymous to help people deal with alcoholism. Their program is one of the most effective in changing people from dependence on alcohol to sobriety. Alcoholics

---

8.   Matthew 6.25, Revised Standard Version of The Bible
9.   Matthew 6.33, Revised Standard Version of The Bible
10. Matthew 6:34, Revised Standard Version of The Bible

Anonymous uses many proven techniques to help reform behaviors including faith in a Higher Power, taking responsibility, verbally confessing to addiction, and encouraging others. One key component, however, requires the recovering alcoholic to strive for abstinence from alcohol one day at a time. The founders knew it might be too overwhelming for an addict to commit to lifetime sobriety. However, by committing to a doable twenty-four hours at a time, by "letting the day's own trouble be sufficient for the day," the recovering alcoholic can make a lifetime change.

In April of 1970, three American astronauts were traveling to the moon. The Apollo spacecraft taking them there was one of the most complex machines built at that time. An explosion on the voyage made landing on the moon impossible and put the very survival of the crew in serious doubt.

Fortunately, the spacecraft was built in three, self-contained units: a service module, a command module, and the lunar landing module. The only way the crew survived the perilous trip back to Earth was by using the undamaged lunar landing module as a lifeboat. They shut down the parts of the ship that were not working properly and focused all of their energies on maximizing the opportunities in the undamaged part of the ship.

When Jesus says, "Don't be anxious about tomorrow...Let the day's own trouble be sufficient for the day" he is advising followers to live in the self-contained compartments. He is instructing us to live for today. We can worry and regret decisions made in the past, but that will not change anything. Worrying about the past will only drain our ability to feel self-assured.

We can also worry and fear things that we might face in the future. Again, worry will not make problems disappear; it will only rob our energies to live abundantly today. What we can do is to learn from the past and plan for the future. What we can control and deal with is the present. Jesus teaches us to live for today.

God declared to Moses, *"I AM WHO I AM."*[11] God did not say the past tense, "I WAS," or the future tense "I WILL BE." The phrase, "I AM," is in the present tense. Followers of God find purpose in keeping his commandments, but we also need to live day by day and acknowledge God as living and active in the present tense.

Developing the loving attitude taught by Jesus is another method to overcome fear and grow in faith. *"There is no fear in love, but perfect love casts out fear. For fear has to do with punishment, and he who fears is not perfected in love."*[12] Fear is a barrier to faith, yet building faith helps overcome fear. Yielding to fear puts one into a downward cycle of doubt and despair while building faith can help conquer fear. Pain, punishment, scarcity, and misery occur when we are physically deprived of something. The spiritual person realizes the suffering in the physical world is only a temporary inconvenience. Our hope should be in the eternal.

Application

Spiritual renewal begins with and cannot occur without faith in God. The prophet Isaiah wrote, *"Have you not known? Have you not heard? The Lord is the everlasting God, the Creator of the ends of the earth. He does not faint or grow weary, his understanding is unsearchable. He gives power to the faint, and to him who has no might he increases strength. Even youths shall faint and be weary, and young men shall fall exhausted; but they who wait for the Lord shall renew their*

---

11. Exodus 3:14, Revised Standard Version of The Bible
12. I John 4:18, Revised Standard Version of The Bible

strength, they shall mount up with wings like eagles, they shall run and not be weary, they shall walk and not faint."[13]

Spiritual strength stems from God. We have authority and responsibility for ourselves, but God is authority for all things. Belief is the beginning of spiritual renewal. Our challenge is to overcome the experiences of constraint and terminality we encounter in the physical world. Our hope is to have faith in the infinite, eternal reunion with God the Father and Creator. Spiritual revival is nurtured in the belief we are created in God's image.

Do not let worry and fear sap your energies toward making good decisions and doing good deeds. The transformed mind overcomes fear by setting God as your purpose, aligning your will with his, becoming more selfless and less selfish, and living one day at a time. To overcome fear and worry,

Learn from the past, Plan for the future, Live for today!

---

13. Isaiah 40:29-31, Revised Standard Version of The Bible

Faith in Action

"Truly, I say to you, whoever says to this mountain, 'Be taken up and cast into the sea,' and does not doubt in his heart, but believes that what he says will come to pass, it will be done for him."

—Jesus Christ, Mark 11:23

In 1974, officials in Osaka, Japan decided to build Kansai International Airport…in the sea. In January 1987, the construction of the fabricated island began. After tons of earth had replaced millions of gallons of seawater, the airport opened on September 4, 1994. Many thought the idea of building an airport in the sea was impractical at best and impossible at worst. Through great effort, focus, and diligence the feat was accomplished. An ancient Chinese proverb says, "He who would move a mountain must begin one stone at a time."

There are limits, of course, to what human beings can accomplish constrained in the physical world. Jesus was talking to his disciples about the difficulty of a rich man entering the kingdom of God; about the difficulty a person has when totally focused on material possessions. He used the analogy that it would be *"easier for a camel to go through the eye of a needle than for a rich man to enter the kingdom of God."*[1] His disciples were concerned. How could any person be saved faced with this type of constraint? Jesus explained, *"…With men this is impossible, but with God all things are possible.*[2] For a person to reach their potential in achievement, in accomplishment, in life, and in spiritual fulfillment, they must believe and rely on God and his omnipotent power.

Belief on its own is not true faith. We have an obligation to put belief in God and the teachings of Jesus into action. Actions are the demonstration of what a person thinks, feels, and believes. We rely on God but we must be committed in our actions to doing his will. The question is asked in the *Book of James*, *"What does it profit, my brethren, if a man says he has faith but has not works? Can his faith save him? If a brother or sister is ill-clad and in lack of daily food, and one of you says to them, 'Go in peace, be warmed and filled,' without giving them the things needed for the body, what does it profit? So faith by itself, if it has no works, is dead."*[3] Transforming belief into faith requires an emotional commitment. *"Faith is the assurance of things hoped for, the conviction of things not seen."* [4]

True, passionate belief is evident in our behavior and in the way we live. Becoming spiritually renewed and finding purpose by drawing close to God means living for God. The writer of the *Letter to the Hebrews* expressed it this way, *"that we may serve the living God!"*[5] God is the **living** God and he should live in the hearts, minds, deeds, and lives of people.

The writer of the *Letter to the Romans* makes a link between living life and serving God. *"Therefore, I urge you, brothers, in view of God's mercy, to offer your bodies as living sacrifices, holy and pleasing to*

1.   Matthew 19:24, Revised Standard Version of The Bible
2.   Matthew 19:26, Revised Standard Version of The Bible
3.   James 2:14-17, Revised Standard Version of The Bible
4.   Hebrews 11:1, Revised Standard Version of The Bible
5.   Hebrews 9:14, New International Version of The Bible

God—this is your spiritual act of worship. Do not conform any longer to the pattern of this world, but be transformed by the renewing of your mind. Then you will be able to test and approve what God's will is—his good, pleasing and perfect will.[6] Putting God in our minds and in our behaviors is the living sacrifice. Living for God is our spiritual act of worship.

The spiritually renewed person must not fit into the mold of the material world, but must be transformed and renewed through the spiritual world in which we hope and believe. Faith moves us to good deeds and righteousness. Belief that does not motivate to action is not faith. The writer of *James* says, *"You believe that God is one; you do well. Even the demons believe that—and shudder."*[7] James also encouraged people to, *"be doers of the word, and not hearers only, deceiving yourselves."*[8] James later says, *"...as the body apart from the spirit is dead, so faith apart from works is dead."*[9]

A person cannot be saved by a faith that does not radically transform their life, conduct, and behavior. True faith will be manifest in actions and works. We are not saved by works, but our actions demonstrate the existence of genuine faith. A true believer will demonstrate faith by a renewed and different character. Paul wrote in his *Second Letter to the Corinthians, "if any one is in Christ, he is a new creation; the old has passed away, behold, the new has come."*[10]

Actions are evidence of faith. As a tree is known by its fruit, good deeds are confirmation of faith. Behaviors and actions have always been more important than words and intentions. The writer of the

---

6. Romans 12:1, 2, Revised Standard Version of The Bible
7. James 2:19, Revised Standard Version of The Bible
8. James 1:22; Revised Standard Version of The Bible
9. James 2:26, Revised Standard Version of The Bible
10. II Corinthians 5:17; Revised Standard Version of The Bible

Letter to the Romans stated, *"it is not the hearers of the law who are righteous before God, but the doers of the law who will be justified."*[11] Jesus made a more chilling proclamation about the importance of actions and obedience to God's will, *"Not every one who says to me, 'Lord, Lord' shall enter the kingdom of heaven, but he who does the will of my Father who is in heaven."*[12]

Application

Imagine that you are commissioned to build a bridge over a deep canyon. You would carefully plan, use the best materials available, and put forth your best effort to build a safe and usable bridge. After construction, you can stand on the brink of the chasm, and say to yourself and others that you believe this to be a good and safe bridge. You may believe in your heart that the bridge is strong, but until you step on the bridge, you are not demonstrating faith. Faith is demonstrated by deeds and actions.

Belief is a powerful force. It begins with possibilities and is demonstrated in actions. Belief in God and his omnipotent power is the foundation of spiritual enlightenment. When we put belief into actions, we align our will with his. When we are living for God by demonstrating his will through actions we can know, *"that all things work together for good to them that love God, to them who are the called according to his purpose."* [13]

We make a myriad of choices everyday. Where we are in life is a result of these individual actions. When we establish God as our purpose, we focus our decisions, actions, and deeds on demonstrating that God is living in us. To be transformed by the renewal of our

11. Romans 2:13; Revised Standard Version of The Bible
12. Matthew 7:21; Revised Standard Version of The Bible
13. Romans 8:28, King James Version of The Bible

mind, we must think right and do the right things. To live righteously…

Do the right things.

The Responsibility to Choose

"If you are unwilling to serve the Lord, choose this day whom you will serve, whether the gods your fathers served in the region beyond the River, or the gods of the Amorites in whose land you dwell; but as for me and my house, we will serve the Lord"

—Joshua, Joshua 24:15

Viktor Frankl, author of the landmark *Man's Search for Meaning* and one of the great psychotherapists of the twentieth century, was a Holocaust survivor of four Nazi death camps, including Auschwitz from 1942–1945.

His parents and other family members died in the camps. Influenced by his horrific experiences in concentration camps, Frankl developed a revolutionary approach to psychotherapy. At the core of his theory was the belief that humanity's primary motivational force is the search for meaning. A person could find personal meaning in life, no matter how dismal the circumstances might be. He wrote of his experiences and said, "Everything can be taken from a man but the last of the human freedoms…to choose one's attitude in any given circumstance, is to choose one's own way."[1] If a person has purpose, they can deal with almost any circumstance.

In teaching personal development classes, I have often used the illustration of Viktor Frankl's concentration camp experiences to emphasize that people have the power to choose their attitude. After one session, a man came up, somewhat emotionally, to hand me a small piece of paper with the German words "Die Gedanken Sind Frei" written on it. I asked him what the words meant. Choking back his emotions, he explained that his mother had been a Holocaust survivor as a young girl. She had taught him this song in German that the prisoners would sing. The words translated mean, "My thoughts are free."

These people, who had survived through the direst of conditions, lived with the fact that everything—property, health, dignity, freedom, and even their lives—could be taken away. Still, they knew the power to choose was theirs.

God has created us with the ability to make moral choices. We are empowered to choose, but with empowerment comes responsibility. According to the *Book of Genesis*, man was made in the image of God. Humankind had dominion to rule over all the creatures of the earth. God even allowed them to choose the names of the many creatures of the creation. God allowed humankind to choose the food to eat and keep the garden with only one commandment, rule, and requirement...to abstain from eating from the tree of the knowledge of good and evil. **Humankind had, and still has, the power of choice.**

Imagine the life of Adam and Eve. They were told three things; be fruitful and multiply, keep the garden, and do not eat of the tree of the knowledge of good and evil. They had only one prohibition.

---

1.   Frankl, Viktor E., Man's Search for Meaning, Washington Square Press, Simon and Schuster, New York, 1963.

They were free to do anything in the garden except eat from the forbidden tree! **Adam and Eve had only one fundamental requirement and command and that was to obey.**

We still, in a way, have one charge to keep, one requirement to please God. We are required to obey. Adam and Eve had the same choice we have today. A simple choice, will we obey God or will we not? This empowerment to choose comes with a price. We are obligated to take responsibility for our choices. Life involves making decisions. We make hundreds of them every day and with choices come consequences and rewards.

Imagine again, Adam and Eve after choosing to disobey God. The command was simple. Eve even quotes the commandment God had given them, *"...You shall not eat of the fruit of the tree which is in the midst of the garden, neither shall you touch it, lest you die."*[2] The temptation began by doubting God, by humankind's arrogance in pitting our will against his, and in believing a lie. The serpent took advantage of this responsibility to choose by telling a lie. To paraphrase the serpent, "You will *not* die! In fact you will be enlightened, you will be as smart as God knowing good and evil."

Good is equal to truth and evil is always associated with lies. The couple ate the fruit because it was attractive to the eye and came with the promise of wisdom. The consequence of disobeying God was death. Paul in his *First Letter to the Corinthians* described the scope of Adam's choice by writing, *"For as in Adam all die, so also in Christ shall all be made alive."*[3]

Other consequences occurred with this act of disobedience.

---

2. Genesis 3:3, Revised Standard Version of The Bible
3. I Corinthians 15:22, Revised Standard Version of The Bible

- **Guilt** *"Then the eyes of both of them were opened, and they realized they were naked; so they sewed fig leaves together and made coverings for themselves. Then the man and his wife heard the sound of the LORD God as he was walking in the garden in the cool of the day, and they hid from the LORD God among the trees of the garden."*[4]

- **Fear** *"But the LORD God called to the man, 'Where are you?' He answered, 'I heard you in the garden, and I was afraid because I was naked; so I hid.'"*[5]

- **Denial and blame** *"'Who told you that you were naked? Have you eaten from the tree that I commanded you not to eat from?' The man said, 'The woman you put here with me—she gave me some fruit from the tree, and I ate it.'"*[6]

- **Death** Although Adam and Eve were not immediately struck down; death soon became a part of their existence. *"And the Lord God made for Adam and for his wife garments of skins, and clothed them."*[7] In an attempt to hide their nakedness, Adam and Eve constructed clothes by sewing fig leaves together. When God made them clothes from the skins of dead animals, it is possibly the first experience the two had with death. The couple also experienced the sorrow of death when their son Cain took the life of his brother Abel in *Genesis 4:8*.

Guilt, fear, denial, blame, and death were all consequences of sin and disobeying God. We live with those same consequences today

---

4.   Genesis 3:7, 8, New International Version of The Bible
5.   Genesis 3:9, 10, New International Version of The Bible
6.   Genesis 3:11, 12, New International Version of The Bible
7.   Genesis 3:21, New International Version of The Bible

when we disobey. Our quest for righteousness and spiritual fulfill-ment is challenged by the same temptation that faced Adam and Eve. James wrote, *"Let no one say when he is tempted, 'I am tempted by God'; for God cannot be tempted with evil and he himself tempts no one; each person is tempted when he is lured and enticed by his own desire. Then desire when it has conceived gives birth to sin; and sin when it is full-grown brings forth death."*[8]

Like Adam and Eve, we typically look for someone to blame beside ourselves when we disobey. They blamed the serpent; we have found a multitude of things to blame. We blame society, our community, families, churches, economic conditions, or our back-ground. The fact is, God created us with the ability and power to choose and with this empowerment comes responsibility. Human-kind's purpose should be focused on God's will. Spiritual renewal happens when we choose to obey God and to align our will with his.

James also wrote, *"Submit yourselves therefore to God. Resist the devil and he will flee from you. Draw near to God and he will draw near to you."*[9] A higher power exists that is in control of things beyond our authority. That higher power is the Creator of the universe, God. When we believe this truth, we are starting our journey toward spir-itual enrichment. Our lives are a result of the choices we have made. Our primary choice in life must be to obey God.

Life is about making choices, about consequences and rewards. A building is made of individual bricks and the quality of the structure depends on the quality of the brick. A person's life is constructed of individual actions or choices a person makes during the course of their life. The quality of a person's life depends on the quality of

---

8.   James 1:13-15, Revised Standard Version of The Bible
9.   James 4:7,8, Revised Standard Version of The Bible

their choices. Doing the right thing is not always easy, but it is always the right thing to do.

The difficulty with choices is the reinforcements (those consequences and rewards) are not always immediate. The affects of the choices, however, are sure.

When I received my first driver's license, it recorded my vital statistics as height-5 foot 10 inches, eyes-green, weight-135 pounds. This information was all correct at age sixteen, but a trip to the doctor at age 42 revealed a height of 5 foot 10 inches, green eyes, and a weight of 228 pounds! An ideal weight would be about 180 pounds. Like many others, I had transformed from a too skinny teenager into a too plump adult. This transformation happened by choices. The decisions I made in eating and the decisions I made in exercise (or the lack of it) were manifest in a slightly overweight, out of condition adult.

These choices in diet and exercise rarely had any immediate consequences. Yes, occasionally I would eat too much and have heartburn, and every two or three years my waist size increased, but eating what I wanted tasted good and made me feel (at least in the short-term) satisfied. The lack of exercise also demonstrated no immediate punishment. In fact, refraining from exercise resulted in no heavy breathing, no sore muscles, and very little sweat. In the short-term, overeating and under exercising presented no consequences but even seemed to have rewards.

The doctor, however, burst my bubble by explaining the consequences of 42 years of eating what I wanted, when I wanted, while not exercising. He explained that a man my age needed to eat a balanced diet and exercise regularly. The consequences, he continued, might include future heart problems, diabetes, a shorter life, and most certainly a poorer quality of life. The consequences for my eating and exercising were sure, although they were taking decades to be revealed.

The doctor convinced me to make changes. Getting someone to change behaviors is a monumental task. He persuaded me to alter my eating habits and begin exercising by explaining the consequences of my past behavior. Dieting and getting into an exercise routine had its own challenges. Changing behaviors and establishing better habits would have its rewards, but just like the consequences, the rewards were not immediate.

I discovered I did a lot of habit eating and used eating to take my mind off other stressful situations. Exercising was uncomfortable and worst of all, the daily trips to the scales showed that the weight was not coming off very fast. Some days I would even gain weight! I had to remind myself that the consequences of bad eating habits and no exercise had not been immediate and the rewards for a better diet and exercising would also be delayed. It had taken twenty-five years to get out of shape; it would take more than a week to get back into shape. Consequences and rewards do not always give us immediate feedback to our choices but at some point, they will most assuredly affect us.

Choices, with their consequences and rewards, affect much more than our physical health, our material wealth, and our social relationships. Choices influence our spiritual self and our relationship with God the Father. The freedom and power given to us by God to make choices comes with great responsibility. We are responsible for our actions, our attitude, and even our thoughts.

Some decisions can and do affect our lives right now while other thoughts, attitudes, and actions may be hidden, disguised, and dormant for a long period of time. It is sometimes easy to fall into the trap of thinking we are getting away with choices that are not coupled with God's will, but we will ultimately be accountable for all the decisions of life.

Application

The conclusion of Solomon's search for spiritual meaning in *Ecclesiastes* gives a chilling look at the magnitude of our responsibility to choose wisely. He writes, *"For God will bring every deed into judgment, with every secret thing whether good or evil."*[10] We have authority over our thoughts and actions. We are also responsible for the choices we make and we will be held accountable to God for those choices. The consequences and rewards for the choices we make will be ours as well.

It is easy to make excuses, to rationalize our behavior, or to blame outside circumstance for the status of our life. It is easy to become more comfortable living a fantasy than dealing with reality. Our spiritual relationship with God will have consequences or rewards. Jesus said, *"Nothing is covered up that will not be revealed, or hidden that will not be known."*[11]

Take responsibility for choices you make.

---

10. Ecclesiastes 12:14, Revised Standard Version of The Bible
11. Luke 12:2, Revised Standard Version of The Bible

An Attitude of Choice

"For as he thinks within himself, so he is."

—Solomon, Proverbs 23:7

One of the most important things we choose in life is our attitude. Attitude is a manner of thinking and feeling, which ultimately dictates our actions and behaviors. Jesus included this concept of personal responsibility to choose one's thoughts and attitudes in many of his teachings. Solomon's proverb paraphrased, "As a person thinks in their heart, so they are," is an enlightened description of a person's character. Character is the sum of all a person thinks.

Jesus addresses the responsibility people have to control their thoughts in his Sermon on the Mount. In the fifth chapter of the *Gospel of Matthew*, Jesus discusses the true challenge of living a spiritual life versus a worldly life. Jesus says, *"You have heard that it was said to the men of old, 'You shall not kill; and whoever kills shall be liable to judgment.' But I say to you that every one who is angry with his brother shall be liable to judgment."*[1]

The tangible action, "do not kill" was one of the Ten Commandments and is a universally accepted rule of human behavior with

---

1. Matthew 5:21, 22, Revised Standard Version of The Bible

almost all societies and groups. For most normal people, this is an easy commandment to keep. Jesus, however, points out that the act of murder begins with the angry attitudes and destructive thoughts a person has for another person. The action is important but the attitude and motivation behind the action may be even more important.

Like the act of murder, adultery is another of God's prohibitions. Some, however, seem to have a more lenient attitude about keeping this commandment. Jesus was clear about his thoughts of purity in marriage. He said, *"Have you not read, that He who created them from the beginning made them male and female, and said, 'For this cause a man shall leave his father and mother, and shall become one flesh?' Consequently they are no longer two, but one flesh. What therefore God has joined together, let no man separate."*[2]

Trust and fidelity are essential ingredients to a long-term relationship. According to Jesus, the act of adultery is so serious, that it is the sole reason for breaching the marriage bond. Jesus concluded his thoughts on marriage and adultery by saying, *"I say to you, whoever divorces his wife, **except for immorality**, and marries another woman commits adultery."*[3] To Jesus, purity in a marriage is imperative and the tangible act of adultery can cause irreparable damage to a marriage relationship.

The physical act of adultery, according to the teachings of Jesus, has its genesis in the mind of humankind. Jesus speaks again in the *Gospel of Matthew* about the importance of attitude in living righteously. *"You have heard that it was said, 'You shall not commit adultery.' But I say to you that every one who looks at a woman lustfully has already committed adultery with her in his heart."*[4]

---

2.   Matthew 19:4-6, Revised Standard Version of The Bible
3.   Matthew 19:9, Revised Standard Version of The Bible
4.   Matthew 5:27, 28, Revised Standard Version of The Bible

The physical act of adultery begins with the mental thoughts of adultery. A man or a woman begins to be unfaithful when they start to think immorally. To effectively do the right things we must think the right things. We are what we do, but we do what we think. To obey God and fully align our will with his, we must work on the mental thoughts or attitudes of the heart. The writer of the *Letter of James* expands the idea that thoughts and desires are the seed of human behavior. *"Let no one say when he is tempted, 'I am tempted by God'; for God cannot be tempted with evil and he himself tempts no one; but each person is tempted when he is lured and enticed by his own desire. The desire when it has conceived gives birth to sin; and sin when it is full-grown brings forth death."*[5] The battle for spiritual righteousness may be manifest in actions, but begins with thoughts, desires, and attitudes of the mind.

One of the keys to a rewarding, spiritually centered life filled with purpose is the discipline to think right and to properly monitor one's attitude. James Allen, the English philosopher and author of the late 19th and early 20th centuries wrote in *As a Man Thinketh*, "The aphorism, 'as a man thinketh in his heart, so is he,' embraces the whole of a man's being. It is so comprehensive that it reaches out to every condition and circumstance of life. A man is literally what he thinks. His character is the sum of all his thoughts."

Allen continued his thoughts on a person's responsibility to choose thoughts and attitudes by saying, "Act is the blossom of thought, and joy and suffering are its fruits; thus a man harvests the sweet and bitter fruits of his own husbandry. Of all the beautiful truths pertaining to the soul, none is more gladdening or fruitful of divine promise and confidence than this—that man is the master of

---

5.   James 1:13-15, Revised Standard Version of The Bible

thought, the molder of character, and the maker and shaper of condition, environment, and destiny."[6]

The choices we make in life will define our character. Our quality of life will also depend on those choices. However, the actual choices we make may not be as important as the motivations, attitudes, and thoughts behind those actions. Thoughts and attitudes are the seeds of choice and actions.

Attitudes are learned responses to how people view, interpret, and believe what they perceive as reality. The simplistic view of attitude is to categorize people as positive or negative attitude people. People with an optimistic outlook are generally characterized as positive while people with a more pessimistic outlook are seen as negative.

The inner thinking and functioning of the human mind, however, is infinitely more complex than simply positive or negative. A multitude of feelings and circumstances affect our ability to have a constructive, positive, and optimistic outlook. There is a continuum of various feelings from positive to negative. A person's character, maturity, and self-assurance are manifest in this great in-between of attitude.

A person's outlook or mental feeling will depend on a variety of outside influences. The negative and selfish attitudes are very much rooted in the carnal, perishable nature of the physical world while the positive and selfless attitudes reflect the more enlightened nature of a spiritual hope. A person must consciously choose to have a more positive and a more selfless attitude, regardless of the circumstance.

Paul described the selfless attitude of Jesus Christ in his *Letter to the Philippians*. *"Your attitude should be the same as that of Christ Jesus: Who, being in very nature God, did not consider equality with God some-*

---

6.   Allen, James, "As A Man Thinketh", 1904

thing to be grasped, but made himself nothing, taking the very nature of a servant, being made in human likeness. And being found in appearance as a man, he humbled himself and became obedient to death—even death on a cross!"[7]

When we choose an attitude of selflessness and put the needs of others before our own needs, we come closer to following the example of Jesus. Treat others, as you would like them to treat you.

Spiritual renewal happens in the thoughts and attitudes of a believer's mind. Paul again writes in his *Letter to the Ephesians*, *"Put off your old nature which belongs to your former manner of life and is corrupt through deceitful lust, and be renewed in the spirit of your minds, and put on the new nature, created after the likeness of God in true righteousness and holiness."*[8] Spiritual renewal requires controlling our thoughts and minds by choosing a more positive, selfless, and constructive attitude.

Application

Circumstances often defeat people **when they believe they are controlled by outside conditions.** However, when we realize the creative control we have over our thoughts, we can begin to realize the new possibilities of spiritual renewal. We are responsible for our actions, and we are responsible for the thoughts we put in our minds. The thoughts of a person will dictate the behavior like the rudder of a ship.

Thought and character are as one. Actions define who we are, but these demonstrations of our true nature are rooted in the attitudes of

---

7. Philippians 2:5-8, Revised Standard Version of The Bible
8. Ephesians 4:22-24, Revised Standard Version of The Bible

the mind. To effectively control our lives we must be in control of our thoughts.

Paul in his *Letter to the Philippians* coached people on how to transform their thinking by advising, *"Whatsoever things are true, whatsoever things are honest, whatsoever things are just, whatsoever things are pure, whatsoever things are lovely, whatsoever things are of good report: if there be any virtue, and if there be any praise, **think on these things.**"* You can greatly affect your attitude by positive thoughts and thinking about the right things.

Improve your attitude by filling your mind with thanksgiving instead of resentment. Look for the good in circumstances instead of expecting the worst. Act enthusiastically about the possibilities in life to serve others and you will find your apathy for life disappears. A positive attitude toward others and an optimistic outlook toward life is choice we can make. Choose your attitude and transform your mind to a more positive state when you choose to,

Count Your Blessings.

---

9.   Philippians 4:8, Revised Standard Version of The Bible

The Opportunity to Change Begins with a Sense of Reality

"There is a way which seems right to a man, but its end is the way to death."

—Solomon, Proverbs 14:12

Physical pain is a harsh reality in nature's learning process. Aristotle said, "We cannot learn without pain." Discomfort is involved in most training, and behaviors are often learned as people try to avoid pain.

Likewise, the problems and conflicts people encounter in their emotional and spiritual life are often symptoms that change needs to occur. Until a person feels the pain, corrective actions or attempts to avoid the pain, will typically not take place. Learning requires a change in behavior and change usually comes with some level of pain and discomfort.

One of the biggest challenges to spiritual renewal is callousness. Paul, in writing about false doctrine in the church, says, *"Speaking lies in hypocrisy; having their conscience seared with a hot iron."*[1] Paul describes people who have lost their sense of right and wrong; people no longer troubled by falsehood. Like scar tissue that has lost the

---

1. I Timothy 4:2, King James Version of The Bible

sensation of touch by being seared, they do not feel the pain of vio-
lating the truth. Paul also wrote, *"They have become callous and have
given themselves up to licentiousness, greedy to practice every kind of
uncleanness."*[2]

The physical senses of hearing, sight, touch, taste, and smell give
feedback and protection from the dangers surrounding us everyday.
We depend on the feelings of pain, sights, and sounds to detect dan-
ger. Even the senses of smell and taste can help protect us from
harm. If any of the five physical senses become dull, the consequences can be disastrous.

In 1968, a woman in London, England awoke one morning to light
her gas stove and put on a kettle of tea. She was battling a sinus infection that severely reduced her sense of smell. Generally, having one's
sense of smell diminished is not a dangerous thing, but on this morning, gas had collected in her kitchen. Gas her nose could not sense.
The subsequent explosion caused the collapse of a multi-story section
of an apartment building resulting in the deaths of many people.
Functioning with dull senses can have catastrophic consequences.

Robert Wadlow was probably the tallest man of the twentieth
century. Born in 1918, he was 7 feet 4 inches tall at the age of 13! By
age 22, he stood an astonishing 8 feet 11 inches. His giant size was
attributed to an overactive pituitary gland for which there was no
medical treatment at the time. Robert had enjoyed good health for
most of his life and had led a relatively ordinary existence, consider-
ing his extraordinary size. He had been in the Boy Scouts, and he
worked for a shoe company traveling the country to display his enormous shoes. His father cut the front seat out of the family car so
Robert could ride in relative comfort while sitting in the back seat.

---

2.   Ephesians 4:19, Revised Standard Version of The Bible

In 1939, the father and son team traveled over 300,000 miles by car to shoe stores across the country.

Robert's large size, 8 feet 11 inches and 490 pounds, left him with little sensation in his feet. This seemed like a blessing at first, since the strain on those feet was great. Unfortunately for Robert, he did not feel the chafing and blistering on his feet until he developed a fatal infection. A routine blister, something that could have been easily treated if he had felt the pain, cost Robert Wadlow his life at the age of only 22. Being callous to pain and discomfort is a dangerous condition physically and a perilous condition spiritually. Pain is a signal to the physical body that changes need to occur.

Besides the physical senses, people have the intuitive sense of right and wrong, which is often described as our conscience. The conscience of an individual can be a devious sense to interpret. When people defy their conscience, they are most certainly wrong, but when they follow their conscience, they may still be off the mark, if they have not developed the right values. A conscience numbed to right and wrong is as spiritually dangerous as walking on top of a high cliff without the physical senses of sight, sound, and touch.

The conscience is a wonderful tool for revealing when we are wrong, but it is not as well equipped to tell us when we are right. A person seeking spiritual renewal will need to develop measures and standards to help them develop objectivity. They will need to test themselves with God's word to ensure their sense of right and wrong is keeping them spiritually centered.

In a spiritual sense, callousness is a significant challenge. People generally do not change from being Godly to godlessness instantaneously. The change happens over time as they become desensitized to the pain associated with disobeying God. Consequences should help condition people to make better choices but sometimes we get insensitive to those consequences. Pain is a signal to change. When a person can no longer feel the pain, it becomes a dangerous situation.

Another challenge in realizing that we need to make changes for spiritual renewal is an inability to have a sense of reality. When we think of visionary people, we often think of people who can "see" the future and determine the way things are going to be. Spiritually successful people must first develop the ability to see the current reality, to see situations for what they really are. We do not always see things as they are, but as we think they are.

Old Testament prophets (people who were able to see the future) would certainly be considered visionary. Most of their writings, however, were not about predicting the future as much as telling about the current conditions. Their writings focused on exposing the current reality, as well as forecasting future events or consequences.

Developing a sense of reality (or seeing things the way they really are) is not a simple task. It requires diligence and effort. There are numerous barriers to our sense of reality including pride, prejudice, time, selfishness, and objectivity.

Sometimes we are so close to the action it becomes difficult to see the whole situation because we lack perspective. Try holding a coin about one inch from your eye and read the date. Most people will be able to see the coin but will not be able to focus on the date *because they are too close*.

My son Jason played center on his freshmen football team. No one pays much attention to the center of the football team, except the parents of the child. A child playing a sport significantly changes a parent's perspective. Jason would hike the ball then dissolve into the tangle of bodies on the line of scrimmage. When talking to him after the game, it was always interesting to compare his perspective on the field with my perspective as a parent in the stands.

If you have ever watched a football game from ground level, particularly from the end zone, you have seen what mass confusion a football game can be. Players on the field actually see very little of the game once the ball is snapped. They see their perspective and the job they are assigned. Few football players call their own plays on the field anymore. The play calling is usually not even done from the sidelines. The coach with the best vision is the coach in the press box. That coach is far enough away to have the best perspective. Many times, we make choices having serious and painful consequences. When we are too close to the action, it becomes difficult to see the way out or to see our opportunities to change.

King David, described as a "man after God's own heart," was a victim of a calloused conscience. His inability to see things for what they were damaged his kingdom and his relationship with God. David saw a woman who was not his wife and chose to have her. To cover up this indiscretion, he tried to manipulate one of his soldiers. When the soldier refused to be manipulated, David conspired to have him killed. All of these actions were consequences of the choice David made to have Bathsheba.

David violated many of God's commandments. Amazingly, he does not seem distraught or repentant. David did not see the consequences of his actions until the prophet Nathan told him a parable.

The LORD sent Nathan to David. He came to him, and said to him, "There were two men in a certain city, the one rich and the other poor. The rich man had very many flocks and herds, but the poor man had nothing but one little ewe lamb, which he had bought. And he brought it up, and it grew up with him and with his children; it used to eat of his morsel, and drink from his cup, and lie in his bosom, and it was like a daughter to him. Now there came a traveler to the rich man, and he was unwilling to take one of his own flock or herd to prepare for the wayfarer who had come to him, but he took the poor man's lamb, and prepared it for the man who had come to him." David's anger was greatly kindled against the man; and he said to Nathan, "As the LORD lives, the man who has done this deserves to die; and he shall restore the lamb fourfold, because he did the thing, and because he had no pity." Nathan said to David, "You are the man." [3]

David, like many of us, knew the consequences of his choices. Like us, he was able to rationalize those choices and blind himself from seeing the pain involved with those choices. David could see clearly in Nathan's parable the right thing to do, but was blind to his own incredible situation.

David was able to desensitize himself from the pain and consequences of his actions. Pain has its purpose, to let the physical body know when to change actions. The pain of a sprained ankle tells the injured person the ligaments are damaged and to quit using the ankle until it can heal. Failing to feel pain can have disastrous affects on a person physically and can have even greater consequences to a person's spiritual health.

David was given the opportunity to change and to repent from his bad choices. He still lived with many of the consequences of the actions, but he did reconcile himself with God and experienced spiritual renewal.

Jesus admonished followers to, *"Judge not, that you be not judged. For with the judgment you pronounce you will be judged, and the measure you give will be the measure you get."* [4] He warns of the tendency humankind has to be critical of others while being blind to our own shortcomings. Jesus continues by asking, *"Why do you see the speck*

---

3.   II Samuel 12:1-7, Revised Standard Version of The Bible
4.   Matthew 7:1,2, Revised Standard Version of The Bible

that is in your brother's eye, but do not notice the log in your own eye?"[5] This teaching warns about trying to judge the motivations and heart of another person, but the teaching also demonstrates the inherent difficulty in analyzing and monitoring our own lives. Developing a good sense of reality, takes effort and courage.

Application

Pain, problems, and conflicts are often symptoms that change needs to occur. Ignoring these signals and numbing ourselves from the pain, can have dangerous consequences. As the physical senses help protect our physical bodies, a keen sense of reality can be a useful tool for spiritual health.

Jesus said, *"The eye is the lamp of the body. So, if your eye is sound, your whole body will be full of light; but if your eye is not sound, your whole body will be full of darkness. If then the light in you is darkness, how great is the darkness!"*[6] Seeing the current situation and having a good sense of reality is essential to spiritual renewal. We all have the opportunity to change, but repentance requires that we see the need to change and realign our will with God. Analyze your life. What types of discomforts are you facing? Are you living with God as the center and purpose of your life or are you living for self? Analyze your feelings, behaviors, and attitudes and

Create a better future, by creating a clear vision of the current reality.

---

5.   Matthew 7:3, Revised Standard Version of The Bible
6.   Matthew 6:22,23, Revised Standard Version of The Bible

The Residual Effect

"...I say unto thee, except a man be born again, he cannot enter into the kingdom of God"

—Jesus, John 3:3

Anyone shoveling snow or ice understands the concept of residual effect. The purpose of removing the frozen material is partly for today, but more importantly for the next few days. The fresh snow and ice may be a hazard, but it is not nearly as dangerous as the melting and refreezing that will occur after the storm.

When snow and ice fall, it can cause problems. If the weather warms however, things can return to normal quickly. If a person neglects to shovel snow, the residual effect of slick sidewalks, impassable driveways, and treacherous roadways last only a few days. In colder climates however, snowstorms are more frequent and stay around longer. The residual effect of not clearing your drive can stay with you the whole winter. Failing to clear the walkway and driveway can leave huge, frozen ruts that become a hazard at best and impassable at worst. The longer one waits to clear the frozen debris, the harder the job of cleaning it off becomes.

One of the few domestic duties I am qualified to do is to iron my dress shirts. Over the years, I have learned the technique and have discovered I like a little starch on the shirts. Over time, the spray starch has a tendency to clog. The instructions on the container tell you to "clean the residue away." Like the residue we experience in physical terms, we must also learn to clean the residue of our spiritual lives. Fortunately, God offers us that possibility. God gives us the opportunity to change.

We are responsible for the choices in our lives. Those choices have a residual effect on the physical, material, and spiritual aspects of our existence.

Many health problems are a result of this residual effect. A person becomes overweight, not by one enormous meal, but by the residual effect of overeating over time. The residue of a person's eating habits affect the digestive system, the circulatory system, the muscle structure, and many other bodily systems.

The residual effect can also affect the economic status of a person. Fortunes are rarely made or lost by one transaction. People generally do not become bankrupt because of one bad purchase. The wealth or poverty of an individual is usually the result of their lifestyle and the many financial choices they make.

Spiritual health and well-being are also subject to residual effect. Spirituality is the essence of a person's mind and heart; the thoughts, attitudes, values, and beliefs a person carries with them. Although the mind of a person is an internal function, it is constantly influenced by external stimulus. We have the responsibility for our thoughts, attitudes, values, and beliefs, but the constant influence of external factors can and does leave a residue.

Computer programmers use an acronym called "GIGO," which stands for Garbage In, Garbage Out. The effectiveness of a computing machine depends on the quality of information put into it. People are also inputting information into their minds by the books they read, the movies they watch, the music they listen to, and the thoughts they think. Wholesome thinking leads to integrity while bad thoughts lead to a corrupted character.

Every experience a human being has, whether positive or negative, leaves a residue. To achieve spiritual purity, it is often necessary to clean away the residue and begin again. One of the great blessings God has given to the beings created in his image is the opportunity to change.

The New Testament word for spiritual change is repentance. The parable of the Prodigal son or lost son is perhaps the greatest teaching about the opportunities of repentance and God's attitude toward the person willing to change.

> *There was a man who had two sons; and the younger of them said to his father, "Father, give me the share of property that falls to me." And he divided his living between them. Not many days later, the younger son gathered all he had and took his journey into a far country, and there he squandered his property in loose living. And when he had spent everything, a great famine arose in that country, and he began to be in want. Soon he went and joined himself to one of the citizens of that country, who sent him into his fields to feed swine. And he would gladly have fed on the pods that the swine ate; and no one gave him anything. But when he came to himself he said, "How many of my father's hired servants have bread enough and to spare, but I perish here with hunger! I will arise and go to my father, and I will say to him, 'Father, I have sinned against heaven and before you; I am no longer worthy to be called your son; treat me as one of your hired servants.'" And he arose and came to his father. But while he was yet at a distance, his father saw him and had compassion, and ran and embraced him and kissed him. And the son said to him, "Father, I have sinned against heaven and before you; I am no longer worthy to be called your son." But the father said to his servants, "Bring quickly*

the best robe, and put it on him; and put a ring on his hand, and shoes on his feet; and bring the fatted calf and kill it, and let us eat and make merry; for this my son was dead, and is alive again; he was lost, and is found." And they began to make merry.[1].

The Prodigal son made his choices and turned away from the wisdom, wealth, and security of his father. In a foreign land, he endures the residual effect of his actions. After despair and suffering, he realizes the consequences of his choices and humbly decides to change, to repent, and come back to the father. He did not expect to be a son again. His guilt and his shame led him to believe he was worthy to be a hired servant but not a son. Repentance is rewarded when the father welcomes and celebrates the lost son's return and his willingness to change the decisions and direction of his life.

Many today relived the story of the Prodigal son. People decide to turn away from God, sometimes completely, but generally in small increments so they can easily rationalize their choices. People do, after all, have free choice and the responsibilities for those choices. The residual effects and the consequences of those choices sometimes cause despair and suffering to a point that one realizes change must occur. God always gives us the opportunity to change, but we have to realize the need for it. Like the father of the Prodigal son, God allows us to always turn back to him and realign our purpose with his will.

Recently, I heard a radio announcer talking about losing weight. She had lost 105 pounds over the last 18 months! The announcer went on to state her goal this year was to lose the last twenty pounds. You would think that would be a very easy task after losing 105

---

1. Luke 15:11-24, Revised Standard Version of The Bible

pounds but she went on to state, "the last twenty pounds were the most difficult to lose."

In a spiritual sense, many struggle with losing the last twenty pounds. In the story of the Prodigal, the lost son was far away and unable to remove the residual effects of his bad decisions by his own efforts. He reached a point of such despair that he gave up, changed his ways, and came a long way home to the father. It is sometimes easier to embrace spiritual change when the distress, despair, and pain of a ruined life bring us to repentance.

Ironically, making needed changes to one's spiritual attitude can be more difficult when a person is deceived into thinking they are righteous. Jesus concluded his tale of the Prodigal son by describing the thinking and attitude of the elder son.

> Now his elder son was in the field; and as he came and drew near to the house, he heard music and dancing. And he called one of the servants and asked what this meant. And he said to him, "Your brother has come, and your father has killed the fatted calf, because he has received him safe and sound." But he was angry and refused to go in. His father came out and entreated him, but he answered his father, "Lo, these many years I have served you, and I never disobeyed your command; yet you never gave me a kid, that I might make merry with my friends. But when this son of yours came, who has devoured your living with harlots, you killed for him the fatted calf!" And he said to him, "Son, you are always with me, and all that is mine is yours. It was fitting to make merry and be glad, for this your brother was dead, and is alive; he was lost, and is found."[2]

This second character in the Prodigal story, the elder son, also lived with the residual effects of an unforgiving attitude. This dili-

---

2. Luke 15:25-32, Revised Standard Version of The Bible

gent son never wandered far from the father in presence, but had wandered far away in spirit. The challenge for the elder son to change and find spiritual renewal, in many ways, was harder than the change the younger son experienced. The pain and despair were not as great and the callousness of living in spiritual comfort had perhaps desensitized him to the gap between himself and the father. He had a short way to go to find the spirit, the truth, and the mercy of the father, but a long way to go in developing the forgiving attitude of the father.

Asking for spiritual help when you feel you do not need it or when you think and reason in your mind that you are righteous, is a difficult change to make to find enlightenment. Many people become desensitized to God's message when they confuse religion with righteousness.

Jesus discusses another aspect of spiritual change during his discussion with Nicodemus recorded in the *Gospel of John*. *"Truly, truly, I say to you, unless one is born anew, he cannot see the kingdom of God.' Nicodemus said to him, 'How can a man be born when he is old? Can he enter a second time into his mother's womb and be born?' Jesus answered, 'Truly, truly, I say to you, unless one is born of water and the Spirit, he cannot enter the kingdom of God. That which is born of the flesh is flesh, and that which is born of the Spirit is spirit.'"* [3]

This promised renewal is for the spiritual essence of the individual and not a physical regeneration of the flesh. Jesus tells Nicodemus unless one is "born anew" and "born of water and Spirit" they cannot enter or participate in the "kingdom of God." This dialogue teaches that a change of heart and true repentance can remove the residue of a person's past life and experiences.

---

3. John 3:3-8, Revised Standard Version of The Bible

The apostle Paul in recounting his experiences in Damascus writes that Ananias said to him, *"And now why do you wait? Rise and be baptized, and wash away your sins, calling on his name."*[4] Baptism is the putting away of an old life and the transformation to a renewed life. It is a spiritual commitment through Christ to change.

Peter described this transformation through baptism by writing, *"For Christ also died for sins once for all, the righteous for the unrighteous, that he might bring us to God, which he went and preached to the spirits in prison, who formerly did not obey, when God's patience waited in the days of Noah, during the building of the ark, in which a few, that is, eight persons, were saved through water.* **Baptism, which corresponds to this, now saves you,** *not as a removal of dirt from the body but as an appeal to God for a clear conscience, through the resurrection of Jesus Christ."*[5]

Peter eloquently explains the role of baptism in repentance by using the metaphor of Noah's ark. Eight people survived the flood by entering the ark and today's believers are saved by entering baptism, not as a physical washing or a mystical religious act, but as a symbol of a believer's death to the old way of living and regeneration to a new spiritual life. Baptism is symbolic of a burial of the old life, filled with mistakes and hopelessness, and a resurrection to a new life, filled with hope and renewal.

The challenge of our religious and spiritual righteousness is to let God live in us. We should not be conformed to the current realities but we should be transformed by thinking about the possibilities. Belief is manifest in actions, attitude, and choices.

---

4.   Acts 22:16, Revised Standard Version of The Bible
5.   I Peter 3:18-21, Revised Standard Version of The Bible

Spiritual renewal requires belief in God as the Creator, an acceptance of responsibility for our life choices, and the opportunity to change by removing the residual effects of past decisions.

Application

Our lives are a result of the decisions and choices we have made. Those choices all come with some level of consequence and reward. Sin can be defined as disobeying God. John wrote, *"If we say we have no sin, we deceive ourselves, and the truth is not in us."*[6] Regardless of how hard one may try to be righteous and keep God's commandments, we live in the physical world of scarcity, competition, and selfishness. We will make decisions that do not measure up to the goodness of God.

John goes on to write and give us great hope by saying, *"If we confess our sins, he is faithful and just, and will forgive our sins and cleanse us from all unrighteousness."*[7]

Use this opportunity to take responsibility for past actions, choices, and decisions. Admit to mistakes of the past and take comfort that they will be forgiven. Clean away the residue of the past and start living better for God today. You can start with a clean slate and

Begin Again To Live For God.

---

6. I John 1:8, Revised Standard Version of The Bible
7. I John 1:9, Revised Standard Version of The Bible

The Economics of Time

"...he has put eternity into man's mind, yet so that he cannot find out what God has done from the beginning to the end."

—Solomon, Ecclesiastes 3:11

Time is moving, fluid, and democratic. It is defined by sayings like, "Time flies" or "Time marches on." Every human being has 24 hours a day, 168 hours a week, and 8,736 hours a year. Job said, *"Man that is born of a woman is of few days, and full of trouble."*[1]

Time waits for no person. Our days are numbered, not numberless. The rich and the poor have the same amount. The flow of time is constant and sure for both. Besides being democratic, time is perishable. You cannot buy it, sell it, or store it. You can only use it wisely. Since time is scarce and perishable, **it has economic value.**

Water is one of the most abundant resources on earth. It covers three fourths of the earth's surface. The human body can survive only a few days without water. Although essential to human existence, water's abundance makes it relatively cheap. Gold, on the other hand, is one of the most valuable metals in the world. It has some useful characteristics, but a human being can easily survive a

---

1. Job 14:1, Revised Standard Version of The Bible

lifetime without seeing or touching gold. What makes gold so valuable and water so cheap is the economic principle of scarcity.

Time has economic value because it is in short supply. In fact, it is the most limited thing a person possesses because it cannot be replenished and is constantly being consumed. The saying, "There aren't enough hours in the day" is a testament to the fact that time is scarce.

More than anything, time brings change. We may not be able to change the nature of time, but time can change outlooks, attitudes, and character. Most things, including time are fluid and moving, in a constant state of flux and change. Understanding the nature and dynamic of time is essential to using time effectively and dealing with the changes time brings.

Since time is scarce and perishable, it is important to develop techniques to use the time we have wisely. Every day people make choices affecting their lives. With each of these choices, whether good or bad, is the underlying fact that time has been spent. Every day, every hour, every minute, and every second that we use has forever vanished. We keep the memories and experiences, but the opportunities and choices are gone. Time is valuable to us because we instinctively know that it is scarce and perishable.

Have you ever noticed how time seems to accelerate and go by faster as we age? I remember being ten years old and having to wait ten days for Christmas. I would tell my dad, "I just can't wait for Christmas. Ten days is so long." My father would assure me that I could wait and that Christmas would get there when it was time.

I now know those ten days were indeed longer for me than for my father because now I am a dad. The ten days before Christmas are a blur these days. There are many activities and never enough time to get everything done. For a ten-year-old anxiously waiting for

Christmas, ten days is still a long time but for a busy adult, ten days is often not enough time to fulfill all of our commitments.

Time, or at least our experience with time, is constantly accelerating. If you take one year of a person's life and divide it by the age of a person, you get the total life experience of that person. For a one-year-old child, one year is 100% of the total life experience while one year for a ten-year-old child is 10% of their total life experience. When a person is 50, one year is only 2% of that person's total life experience.

What would you do if you knew this was the last day of your life? Would you live it differently? Would you value and appreciate different things? Would your priorities change? The nature and truth about time is that it is constantly moving and taking each person closer to the end of their time.

Time is valuable because it is scarce and it is scarce because we live in a finite, physical world. Every tangible thing that we know and experience is being consumed. The clock is literally ticking.

In the realm of the spiritual, however, time would be viewed much differently. Peter wrote, "*...do not ignore this one fact, beloved, that with the Lord one day is as a thousand years, and a thousand years as one day.*"[2] Without the decaying characteristics of the physical world, the concept of time changes dramatically. If time were in abundance, we would have a much different attitude about what is urgent and what is really important.

David contemplated the contrast between the eternal God and the transitory nature of humankind. His psalm describes the temporal nature of our physical world and the eternal characteristics of our spiritual God.

---

2.   II Peter 3:8, Revised Standard Version of The Bible

Psalms 90

Lord, thou hast been our dwelling place in all generations.

Before the mountains were brought forth,

or ever thou hadst formed the earth and the world,

from everlasting to everlasting thou are God.

Thou turnest man back to the dust,

and sayest, "Turn Back, O children of men!"

For a thousand years in thy sight

are but as yesterday when it is past,

or as a watch in the night.

Thou dost sweep men away; they are like a dream,

like grass which is renewed in the morning:

in the morning it flourishes and is renewed;

in the evening it fades and withers.

For we are consumed by thy anger;

by thy wrath we are overwhelmed.

Thou hast set our iniquities before thee,

our secret sins in the light of thy countenance.

For all our days pass away under thy wrath,

our years come to an end like a sigh.

The years of our life are threescore and ten,

or even by reason of strength fourscore;

yet their span is but toil and trouble;

they are soon gone, and we fly away.

Who considers the power of thy anger,

and thy wrath according to the fear of thee?

So teach us to number our days

that we may get a heart of wisdom.[3]

Jesus declared, *"I came that they may have life, and have it abundantly."*[4] For a life to be abundant, it would need to have unlimited resources. The abundant life focuses on the spiritual nature and not the temporal, physical world. The abundant life is only possible through faith in the promise of Jesus Christ.

Our concept of time as a scarce commodity presents a barrier to spiritual renewal. We must transcend the finite characteristics of the non-renewable physical nature to the infinite promise of eternity through faith in Jesus Christ and his promise.

Application

Time is a dynamic force, continually taking us into the future. Experiences, knowledge, and wisdom can only come through a person's involvement with time. The limited supply of time a person has to live their life, however, makes time a valuable commodity.

We should take account of our days so that we can live each day in God's image, selflessly, obediently, and with purpose. Every moment of every day is precious. Each experience in God's creation is an opportunity to grow in knowledge and understanding. It is an opportunity to gain insights and have an attitude of learning that leads to wisdom. As David concluded in his psalm about the eternal

---

3.   Psalms 90:1-12, Revised Standard Version of The Bible

4.   John 10:10, Revised Standard Version of The Bible

God and transitory man, *"Teach us to number our days that we may get a heart of wisdom."*[5]

Make every moment an opportunity.

---

5.   Psalms 90:12, Revised Standard Version of The Bible

Spiritual Renewal and the Church

"For where two or three are gathered in my name, there am I in the midst of them."

—Jesus, Matthew 18:20

While attending a secular leadership conference several years ago, I was struck by the amount of time, attention, and discussion given to spirituality, moral conscience, and faith. Speakers and writers specializing in the study of leadership had discovered something I had always believed. Faith is important. I was equally struck by the fact that although these people recognized the importance of spiritual development and moral character in leadership, they did not associate organized religion or the church as a necessary tool in spiritual development.

This group of intelligent, scholarly students of leadership reflects the beliefs and attitudes of many today. The opinion of numerous people is that spiritual development is important, but church is not essential. In fact, the church is viewed by some as detrimental to personal and spiritual development!

This gap between the way many feel about spiritual development and the role of the church comes from a basic misunderstanding about the church and its purpose. The church is not a place, a building, an organization, a social club, or an association. The word "church" in the Bible is not used as a name or title and it is not capitalized as a proper noun. The church is a called out assembly. It is a group of people with a common belief in God, and in his son Jesus Christ. The church is spiritual. It is not a place and is not constructed with physical brick and mortar. The church exists in the lives of believers.

Jesus talked about the church to his disciples, *"Now when Jesus came into the district of Caesarea Philippi, he asked his disciples, 'Who do men say that the Son of man is?' And they said, 'Some say John the Baptist, others say Elijah, and others Jeremiah or one of the prophets.' He said to them, 'But who do you say that I am?' Simon Peter replied, 'You are the Christ, the Son of the living God.' And Jesus answered him, 'Blessed are you Simon Bar-Jona! For flesh and blood has not revealed this to you, but my Father who is in heaven. And I tell you, you are Peter, and on this rock I will build my church, and the powers of death shall not prevail against it.'"*[1]

"You are the Christ, the Son of the living God" is or should be the core belief of the church. Jesus specifically says this knowledge was not "revealed by man, but by my Father in heaven." The church by its very nature is spiritual and not material. Jesus goes on to declare that it is "my church." The church belongs to no person, group, organization, convention, or hierarchy. The church belongs only to Jesus Christ, it is his church.

Christ's church, the called out assembly and the spiritual fellowship, has Jesus Christ as the cornerstone. Christ's followers bind together in a common citizenship of God's people. *"So then you are no longer strangers and sojourners, but you are fellow citizens with the saints and members of the household of God, built upon the foundation of*

---

1. Matthew 16:13-18, Revised Standard Version of The Bible

the apostles and prophets, Christ Jesus himself being the cornerstone, in whom the whole structure is joined together and grows into a holy temple in the Lord; in whom you also are built into it for a dwelling place of God in the Spirit.[2]

The church is a group of "fellow citizens" with a "foundation of the apostles and prophets" with Jesus Christ as "the cornerstone" or the chief focus of the group. This select group binds together in a spiritual, not physical, building and holy temple in the Lord. The living God resides in this temple. This group, the church, is built together to become a dwelling in which God lives by his Spirit.

Peter writes about the church being constructed of "living stones." *"Come to him, to that living stone, rejected by men but in God's sight chosen and precious; and like living stones be yourselves built into a spiritual house, to be a holy priesthood, to offer spiritual sacrifices acceptable to God through Jesus Christ."*[3] God lives in the hearts and minds of obedient believers, not in material or physical places.

Jesus was having a casual conversation with a woman of Samaria in the *Gospel of John* when she inquired, *"'Sir, I perceived that you are a prophet. Our fathers worshiped on this mountain; and you say that in Jerusalem is the place where men ought to worship.' Jesus said to her, 'Woman, believe me, the hour is coming when neither on this mountain nor in Jerusalem will you worship the Father. You worship what you do not know; we worship what we know, for salvation is from the Jews. But the hour is coming, and now is, when the true worshipers will worship the Father in spirit and truth, for such the Father seeks to worship him. God is spirit, and those who worship him must worship in spirit and truth."*[4] The woman asked a question about physical geography, but

---

2. Ephesians 2:19-22, Revised Standard Version of The Bible
3. I Peter 2:4, 5, Revised Standard Version of The Bible
4. John 4:19-24, Revised Standard Version of The Bible

Jesus foreshadowed the Kingdom of God, which would reside in the heart, minds, and lives of believers.

The church is spiritual, composed of individuals following Jesus Christ and centering their lives on him. This group can be large and universal, encompassing the whole host of believers, or small and localized. The church is referred to in several localities as in the *Book of Acts*, "*Then the church throughout Judea, Galilee and Samaria enjoyed a time of peace.*"[5] The church is also described in specific localities, like the church at Corinth or the church at Jerusalem. Jesus promised, "*where two or three come together in my name, there am I with them.*"[6]

The beginning of the church is chronicled in the second chapter of the *Book of Acts* immediately after Peter's sermon on the day of Pentecost. It is important to note that Peter and the other apostles were not recruiting people to the church, teaching them about church, or asking them to join the church. They were preaching Jesus Christ, his sacrifice, and his resurrection. The church was a natural result from the gathering of believers in Jesus Christ.

> *Those who accepted his message were baptized, and about three thousand were added to their number that day. They devoted themselves to the apostles' teaching and to the fellowship, to the breaking of bread and to prayer. Everyone was filled with awe, and many wonders and miraculous signs were done by the apostles. All the believers were together and had everything in common. Selling their possessions and goods, they gave to anyone as he had need. Every day they continued to meet together in the temple courts. They broke bread in their homes and ate together with glad and sincere hearts, praising God and enjoying the favor of all the people. And the Lord added to their number daily those who were being saved.*[7]

---

5. Acts 9:31, New International Version of The Bible
6. Matthew 18:20, New International Version of The Bible

Individual members were not added by vote or registration, but by accepting the message of repentance and baptism. The purpose and role of the church was to provide common encouragement, where they could devote "themselves to the apostles teaching and to the fellowship, to the breaking of bread and to prayer."

The church from the beginning was a group of believers in Jesus Christ, bound together to support and encourage one another. People were "built together to become a dwelling in which God lives by his Spirit." The believers were so committed to one another they "had everything in common" giving as any had need. They were meeting together every day, not in empty ritual or from compulsion, but with "glad and sincere hearts."

This group, the called out assembly, was not an exclusive group. "The Lord" added members to the group, the church, "day by day" as they were being saved. The original purpose of the church was to encourage and edify the members. The members met together willingly and gladly to learn, to fellowship, to break bread, and to pray.

We get another glimpse of the early church in the fourth chapter of the *Book of Acts. "All the believers were one in heart and mind. No one claimed that any of his possessions was his own, but they shared everything they had. With great power the apostles continued to testify to the resurrection of the Lord Jesus, and much grace was upon them all."*[8]

It is an extraordinary occurrence to have any group of people "one of heart and mind." This was possible because the church focused on the person of Jesus Christ and his teachings. He was the purpose and the primary focus for the group. The teachings were concentrated on the person of Jesus Christ and his resurrection.

---

7. Acts 2:41-47, New International Version of The Bible
8. Acts 4:32, 33, New International Version of The Bible

The original purpose of the church was the person, teachings, redemption, life, death, resurrection, and hope of Jesus Christ. The believers gathered together willingly to support and encourage those of like faith. The New Testament, however, predicted that the utopian existence of the church would be challenged.

The history of humankind has demonstrated a tendency to have an erosion of purpose. The nation of Israel many times would fall away from their purpose to love and serve God. The New Testament not only warns of churches and Christians falling away, but also documents such events. Paul wrote to Timothy, *"For men will be lovers of self, lovers of money, proud, arrogant, abusive, disobedient to their parents, ungrateful, unholy, inhuman, implacable, slanderers, profligates, fierce, haters of good, treacherous, reckless, swollen with conceit, lovers of pleasure rather than lovers of God, holding a form of religion but denying the power of it. Avoid such people."*[9]

Paul uses harsh language in this warning to Timothy. Words like "proud," "arrogant," "ungrateful," "inhuman," "fierce," are used to describe people who consider themselves religious. He tells Timothy that people will forget the selfless nature of the church and instead become "lovers of self" and that some will have a "form of religion" but not realize the power of belief in Jesus Christ and God.

In the Bible, religion is not always equated with righteousness. In fact, the Bible reveals that humankind has a propensity to exchange God's law for traditions and ritual. Jesus quoted the prophet Isaiah saying, *"This people honors me with their lips, but their heart is far from me; in vain do they worship me, teaching as doctrines the precepts of men."*[10] People who consider themselves religious may need to be

---

9.   II Timothy 3:2-7, Revised Standard Version of The Bible
10. Mark 7:6, 7, Revised Standard Version of The Bible

even more vigilant in monitoring their righteousness, to insure they are living according to God's will and not the wisdom or "precepts" of men.

The nation of Israel continually strayed from the purpose to love God and keep his commandments. The preaching of Jesus consistently targeted the religious leaders of his day. In the 23rd chapter of the *Gospel of Matthew*, Jesus rants about the scribes and Pharisees with their outward adorning of religion but their inward neglect of the "weightier matters of the law."

> *Then Jesus said to the crowds and to his disciples: "The teachers of the law and the Pharisees sit in Moses' seat. So you must obey them and do everything they tell you. But do not do what they do, for they do not practice what they preach. They tie up heavy loads and put them on men's shoulders, but they themselves are not willing to lift a finger to move them. Everything they do is done for men to see."[11]*

Jesus warns about empty rituals done only to impress people. He encouraged his followers to go beyond the religion and ritual of the day by focusing not only on the outward actions of worship but also on the thoughts, attitudes, and motivations of the mind.

Paul, when faced with the philosophy and idolatry of Athens, declared, *"Men of Athens, I perceive that in every way you are very religious."*[12] Paul goes on to give one of the most eloquent theological discourses on monotheism recorded in the Bible. He acknowledged their religiousness then proceeded to teach them about the nature of God by instructing them that religion is not the same as righteousness. Paul continues his definition of true worship by saying,

---

11. Matthew 23:1-5, New International Version of The Bible
12. Acts 17:22, Revised Standard Version of The Bible

For as I passed along, and observed the objects of your worship, I found also an altar with this inscription, "To an unknown god." What therefore you worship as unknown, this I proclaim to you. The God who made the world and everything in it, being Lord of heaven and earth, does not live in shrines made by man, nor is he served by human hands, as though he needed anything, since he himself gives to all men life and breath and everything. And he made from one every nation of men to live on all the face of the earth, having determined allotted periods and the boundaries of their habitation, that they should seek God, in the hope that they might feel after him and find him. Yet he is not far from each one of us, for "In him we live and move and have our being"; as even some of your poets have said, "For we are indeed his offspring." Being then God's offspring, we ought not to think that the Deity is like gold, or silver, or stone, a representation by the art and imagination of man.[13]

Paul's discourse, while standing in the middle of the Areopagus in Athens, addresses the spiritual nature of God the Creator. He also reaffirms that the living God can be experienced and that, "He is not far from each one of us." Although Paul described the Athenians as "very religious," he goes on to explain that being religious and righteous are two different things.

For the church to succeed today in providing spiritual renewal and encouragement, it must constantly be reminded of its purpose, which is to worship God through his son Jesus Christ and to encourage his followers. Believers in Christ, or Christians, must have a common purpose. The church is real, yet invisible. It is constructed of all who believe in Jesus and obey his commands. The church is not brick and mortar; it is a virtual organization. Christ's church is spiritual and living.

---

13. Acts 17:23-29, Revised Standard Version of The Bible

"Just as each of us has one body with many members, and these members do not all have the same function, so in Christ we who are many form one body, and each member belongs to all the others."[14] The church is organic and is compared to a body, formed with many members. The health of the body depends on the health of all the parts. Christians must be encouragers if the church is to serve as the spiritual development instrument Jesus intended it to be.

Paul gives Christians a "to do" list of things required to nourish a church in his *Letter to the Romans*.

> *Let love be genuine; hate what is evil, hold fast to what is good; love one another with brotherly affection; outdo one another in showing honor. Never flag in zeal, be aglow with the Spirit, serve the Lord. Rejoice in your hope, be patient in tribulation, be constant in prayer. Contribute to the needs of the saints, practice hospitality. Bless those who persecute you; bless and do not curse them. Rejoice with those who rejoice; weep with those who weep. Live in harmony with one another; do not be haughty, but associate with the lowly; never be conceited. Repay no one evil for evil, but take thought for what is noble in the sight of all. Beloved, never avenge yourselves, but leave it to the wrath of God; for it is written, "Vengeance is mine, I will repay, says the Lord." No, "if your enemy is hungry, feed him; if he is thirsty, give him drink; for by so doing you will heap burning coals upon his head." Do not be overcome by evil, but overcome evil with good.*[15]

Christ's church must be filled with love. *"Love does no wrong to a neighbor; therefore love is the fulfilling of the law."*[16] Loving and encouraging fellow Christians is living the teachings of Jesus. The

---

14. Romans 12:4, 5, New International Version of The Bible
15. Romans 12:9-21, Revised Standard Version of The Bible
16. Romans 13:10, Revised Standard Version of The Bible

church and its members must vigilantly remember and rededicate themselves to the true purpose of the church.

Application

Jesus, in talking to the religious elite of his day, was questioned about the nature of his kingdom. *"Having been asked by the Pharisees when the kingdom of God would come, Jesus replied, 'The kingdom of God does not come with your careful observation, nor will people say, 'Here it is,' or 'There it is,' because* **the kingdom of God is within you.***"*[17]

The church of Jesus is not built with architectural plans or the finest building materials. It is not filled with symbols and empty ritual. The church Jesus established is to live in the hearts, minds, and actions of the believers. Christ's church is not about opinions confused as truth, rules imposed by others, the wisdom of the current age, or precepts of any man or organization. It is simply the gathering and encouraging of people who have a common purpose of following, living, and hoping in the promises of Jesus Christ.

The church of Christ should have as its primary mission to teach others about the love, the hope, and the wonder of Jesus Christ. It should teach that his sacrifice for humankind's sin is the way to reconcile the physically deteriorating nature with the spiritual promise of renewal through the only Son of God.

For a church to dynamically grow and develop it must be an encouragement to all. To encourage all we must,

Treat others, as we like to be treated.

---

17. Luke 17:20, 21, New International Version of The Bible

Concluding Thoughts

Spiritual renewal requires God to be the focal point. It begins when we acknowledge God as the creator of all things. The power of belief, the responsibility to choose, and the opportunity to change are fundamental to spiritual development.

The path toward spiritual renewal begins by acknowledging and **believing** in God as the purpose and force in our lives. It requires us to accept **responsibility** not only for our actions, but also for our thoughts and attitudes. Spiritual renewal involves a **change** from pursuing the temporal things of the physical world to seeking the promises of a spiritual life.

True genius is to transform the complicated into the simple. The teachings of Jesus are simple, but that does not mean they will be easy. To be spiritually fulfilled, we must become:

- More selfless and less selfish,

- More assured and less fearful,

- More focused on infinite promises of eternity and less on the finite physical nature of life.

The transformed mind thinks differently and more positively to create more peace of mind, more energy, and more satisfaction with life. By centering your life on spiritual abundance instead of physical scarcity, you can renew the spirit within you to think about love, joy, peace, patience, kindness, goodness, faithfulness, gentleness, and self-control. Determining your thoughts and attitude is a choice you can make.

If we live serving God, we will not live without God. Respecting God and keeping his commandments is the "whole duty of man" according to Solomon. The trials, troubles, problems, and conflicts of life are often an indication that change needs to occur. The great gift of God is the opportunity to change.

Draw near to God and He will draw near to you.

Three Essentials to Spiritual Renewal

- The Power of <u>Belief</u>

- The Responsibility to <u>Choose</u>

- The Opportunity to <u>Change</u>

Remember to

- Establish God as your purpose.

- Align your thoughts with God's will.

- Become more selfless and less selfish by developing a loving attitude.

- Say I can…do all things in him who strengthens me.

- Learn from the past, Plan for the future, Live for today!

- Do the right things.

- Take responsibility for choices you make.

- Count your blessings.

- Create a clear vision of a better future, by creating a clear vision of the current reality.

- Begin again, to live for God.

- Make every moment an opportunity.

- Treat others, as we like to be treated.

- Draw near to God and He will draw near to you.

Bibliography

Allen, James, *As A Man Thinketh*, 1904, London

American Foundation for Suicide Prevention, http://www.afsp.org

Frankl, Viktor E., *Man's Search for Meaning*, Washington Square Press, Simon and Schuster, New York, 1963.

Hayes, Mark. *Sooner Rather Than Later*, The Sporting News, January 2001, http://www.sportingnews.com/voices/matt_hayes/20010109.html

Revised Standard Version of the Bible, copyright 1952 [second edition, 1971] by the Division of Christian Education of the National Council of the Churches of Christ in the United States of America. Used by permission. All rights reserved.

Tolstoy, Leo Nikolayevich, *A Confession*, 1879, Russia

King James Version of the Bible

New International Version of the Bible, copyright 1973, 1978, 1984 by International Bible Society. Used by permission. All rights reserved.

Quoted Biblical Passages

Genesis 1:1

Genesis 1:26

Genesis 3:3

Genesis 3:7, 8

Genesis 3:9, 10

Genesis 3:11, 12

Genesis 3:21

Exodus 3:14

II Samuel 12:1-7

I Kings 10:23

Job 14:1

Psalms 90:1-12

Psalms 139:14

Ecclesiastes 1:2, 3

Ecclesiastes 1:14

Ecclesiastes 3:11

Ecclesiastes 12:13

Ecclesiastes 12:14

Isaiah 40:29-31

Matthew 5:21, 22

Matthew 5:27, 28

Matthew 5:43, 44

Matthew 6:22, 23

Matthew 6:25-33

Matthew 6:34

Matthew 7:1,2

Matthew 7:3

Matthew 7:12

Matthew 7:13

Matthew 7:21

Matthew 14:2

Matthew 16:13-18

Matthew 18:20

Matthew 19:4-6

Matthew 19:9

Matthew 19:24

Matthew 19:26

Matthew 22:35-40

Matthew 23:1-5

Mark 5:36

Mark 7:6, 7

Luke 12:2

Luke 15:11-24

Luke 15:25-32

Luke 17:20, 21
John 3:3-8
John 4:19-24
John 6:63
John 10:10
Acts 2:41-47
Acts 4:32, 33
Acts 9:31
Acts 17:22
Acts 17:23-29
Acts 22:16
Romans 2:13
Romans 8:6
Romans 8:28
Romans 8:31
Romans 12:1, 2
Romans 12:4, 5
Romans 12:9-21
Romans 13:8-10
I Corinthians 2:7-11
I Corinthians 2:12
I Corinthians 13:4-7
I Corinthians 15:19
I Corinthians 15:22
II Corinthians 4:16-18
II Corinthians 5:17
Galatians 5:14
Galatians 5:16-23

Ephesians 2:19-22
Ephesians 4:19
Ephesians 4:22-24
Philippians 2:5-8
Philippians 4:8
Philippians 4:11, 12
Philippians 4:13
Colossians 3:10
I Timothy 4:2
II Timothy 3:2-7
II Timothy 3:16
Hebrews 9:14
Hebrews 11:1
Hebrews 11:3
Hebrews 13:6
James 1:13-15
James 1:22
James 2:14-17
James 2:19
James 2:26
James 4:7, 8
I Peter 2:4, 5
I Peter 3:18-21
II Peter 3:8
I John 1:8
I John 1:9
I John 4:12
I John 4:18

0-595-32179-8

LaVergne, TN USA
03 September 2009
156805LV00004B/9/A